OPERA BEFORE MOZART

Michael F. Robinson
MA, B.MUS, D.PHIL

HUTCHINSON U
LO

HUTCHINSON & CO (Publishers) LTD

178–202 Great Portland Street, London W1

London Melbourne Sydney
Auckland Bombay Toronto
Johannesburg New York

★

First published 1966

*Cover design of paperback edition
by courtesy of the Victoria and Albert Museum*

© Michael F. Robinson 1966

*This book has been set in Bembo, printed in Great Britain
on Smooth Wove paper by Anchor Press, and
bound by Wm. Brendon, both of Tiptree, Essex*

CONTENTS

ACKNOWLEDGMENTS

Opera before Mozart owes much to the help of many friends and acquaintances, of whom I should like to mention Denis Arnold, Dennis Arundell, Gwynfor Griffith, Jack Sage, and Merlin Thomas, who have generously given information in their specialist fields. My thanks go also to Simon Towneley, who kindly undertook the task of reading through the manuscript, and to the Research Fund Committee of the University of Durham, who financed some of my many journeys made during this book's preparation.

PREFACE

The length of time between the earliest operas, *c.* 1600, and
Mozart's first mature opera *Idomeneo*, 1781, is little shorter than that
between *Idomeneo* and the present. The title *Opera before Mozart*
therefore embraces the first half of operatic history, and the less
understood half. Since most opera companies select from Mozart
and Gluck onwards, nearly all the operas in the standard current
repertoire are drawn from the second and later period. Sometimes
an earlier work like Monteverdi's *L'incoronazione di Poppea*, 1642,
is revived and accepted by the modern public as both musically and
dramatically satisfying. Handel's operas have enjoyed a vogue for
some time. In view of these revivals it may well be asked what
chances there are for further deserving works to be unearthed and
performed. Operas there are in abundance, but whether the
majority of these would nowadays excite more than polite expressions of interest is another matter. The fact is that concepts of what
constitutes good opera have varied considerably from one period
to the next. While artistic failings in many of the early operas may
be blamed squarely on the librettist or composer, we should also
realise that audience reactions have altered over the years, and that
aesthetic values too have changed.

This adds to the difficulty of assessing many early operas at their
true worth. The assessment cannot be made at all without reference
to the cultural climate of the time, and students of opera may have
to pay more attention in future than many do now to political and
social pressures, to the intellectual atmosphere, and to the arts
other than music, that together affect their subject. This particular

book makes no attempt to cover all the major events or list all the important artists. It is, however, intended to present a microcosm of relevant cultural and external influences, together with as much detailed information about the general course of operatic development as is possible in a work of this size.

I

OPERA AS AN ART-FORM

'No method more effectual', wrote Algarotti at the beginning of his *Essay on the opera* of the year 1755, 'hath been imagined by human invention, to afford a delightful entertainment to ingenious minds, than that all-accomplished and harmonious performance, by way of excellence, called OPERA; because in forming it no article was forgotten . . . that could in any shape contribute to so important an end: and indeed, it may with reason be affirmed, that the most powerful charms of music, of the mimic art, of dancing, and of painting, are in operatic performances all happily combined.'[1] Such words could only have been written by an enthusiast for opera who was in no doubt either about its past and present successes or about its chances of future development. Yet Algarotti was far from complaisant about his subject. His remark about the arts involved was merely an introduction to a strongly worded plea that they should be more intelligently combined in an over-all scheme than was usual in opera of his period.

This combining of various arts in opera has before now led to arguments about the function and exact rating of each. The experience of history seems on the side of those who maintain that music is that superior element which gives perpetual life to some operas and condemns others to extinction. Music in opera is more than a reflection of the other arts involved. It is a new, decisive creation, a fact we acknowledge by our habit of associating operas chiefly with the names of composers. A look at the relationship between music and text in opera will reveal the extent to which the

1. Superior figures refer to bibliographical notes at the end of chapters.

music can affect the artistic character of the whole. The music cannot proceed entirely independently of the text, of course, but it will establish its own pace and emotional atmosphere. Take, for example, the end of Mozart's *Don Giovanni* where everyone sings:

> Questo è il fin di chi fa mal.
> E de'perfidi la morte
> Alla vita è sempre ugual!*

The action has already finished before this moment and the characters are lined up at the front of the stage to draw the moral of the story. The music, however, suggests that the action is still in progress, since it is as lively and boisterous as in previous sections of the work—the end of Act I, for instance—where characters are embroiled in a fast-moving plot. Possibly more solemn music might emphasise the serious nature of these words, but no one is likely to argue nowadays that Mozart's judgment was at fault when he composed this passage or that the scene is dramatically unsatisfactory as it stands.

If opera has usually tended to be a musical art in practice, this is because of the natural assertiveness of the musician to make it a vehicle for his own expression. On the other hand, the creators of the very first operas in Florence and Rome, *c.* 1600, were not aiming primarily to create a drama in which music had pride of place. They were striving, simply, to create drama. Their audiences were not invited to pay particular attention to music but to share in an ideal theatrical experience in which music was admittedly omnipresent but nevertheless kept its place. The theory that music should 'keep its place' was one expressed in various ways at several subsequent periods of operatic history. Its essence was to be found, for example, in Algarotti's *Essay* and much later in Wagner's *Oper und Drama*. Such theory was concerned basically with two things: in the first instance, with the subservience of music to the over-all dramatic scheme; in the second, with the need to allow other constituent elements in opera, the libretto, stage designs, dancing, etc., to play their full part in the work.

Any idea that such theory automatically impeded composers is squashed at once by the examples of Gluck and Wagner. Both set out to make their music serve drama, and both created operas with excellent and highly individual music. Theory prevented neither

*'This is the end of the evil doer. As a man lives, so shall he die!'

from writing what came naturally to him. The danger to opera in general came from those non-musicians who claimed that the various elements should be held in equal balance or that music should be subservient not only to the over-all scheme but to other elements and especially the text. Such ideas could severely hamper a composer if non-musical factions insisted on their rigid application.

Whether different arts had similar and equal functions was a key point of conjecture among artists and intellectuals in the seventeenth and early eighteenth centuries. Many of the most characteristic artistic creations of this period—which historians of the fine arts label in general terms the 'baroque'—display a merger of different elements and a blurring of the functions between them. Baroque altar-pieces, especially in some German churches, may be cited as examples. These are worked in a large variety of building materials, and very often include both painting and sculpture. Although this was complicated enough, the designing of an altar-piece was not an end in itself but an attempt to add yet another factor to the general architectural plan of the church. The figures surrounded by their stucco clouds at the top of the altar lead the eye naturally up to the ceiling where painted figures and cloud formations greet it. These in their turn lead the eye elsewhere. The whole in fact represents one decorative pattern, although many materials and crafts are employed. Another feature of baroque altar-pieces is the arrangement of sculptured or painted figures in histrionic postures. These figures seem ready to spring to life at any moment to enact the Annunciation, St George killing the dragon, or whatever story is concerned. Here again is an overlap of different spheres of artistic expression, in this case between the visual arts and drama.

Now opera is in the baroque period perhaps the baroque art-form *par excellence*, because it employed a maximum number of arts and fitted them all into a combined scheme. The fact that an opera performance was all over after three to five hours—contrasting with the permanent quality of architecture—did not lessen its importance in the eyes of people in the baroque period. For here the architect —who often coupled his duties with those of stage-designer—was joined by the librettist, the composer, singers, ballet dancers and others to create the most complicated art structure imaginable. All in their own way were considered creators in the scheme, so had some claim to be treated as equal partners.

One important point about baroque churches is that ultimate responsibility for the artistic design rested squarely on the architect or small group of architects in charge. Since many of the greatest of these were—like their predecessors of the Renaissance—also expert painters and sculptors, their experience covered a wide range of arts associated with building and their chances of including these successfully were considerable. In the sphere of opera no one was likely to have expert skill in all the artistic branches, though one or two did try to obtain it.* Who then was chiefly responsible and influential in the operatic design?

The short answer is that it was the patrons who could effectively dictate taste and thus place an artist on a pedestal or relegate him to an inferior position. If patrons required elaborate stage machinery and ravishing spectacle—as they did for instance in Rome in the 1630's and in Venice in the 1640's—then elaborate machinery and lavish spectacle there had to be. Yet individual artists could also exert considerable influence, especially since a new opera was usually planned with most of the artists working together on the spot, and since the personality of some was bound to be greater than that of others. We know from Mozart's correspondence how his personal influence affected much more than just the music of *Idomeneo*,[2] and how, on his insistence, sections of the text had to be shortened or changed, and characters' entries rearranged. Quite notorious was the way in which eighteenth-century Italian singers dictated the style and shape of the arias they sang. Other artists could also change the emphasis in favour of their particular art.

Of the various relationships, that between composer and librettist was particularly important. We know something about the theoretical side of this relationship, since the problem of balancing words and music was one that bothered intellectuals and consequently was often mentioned in print. Supported, in general, by the powerful and very articulate literary camp, librettists had a host of weapons to flourish in support of their claim that words mattered most. Included in their arsenal was the popular, classically inspired ideal of the theatre as a type of public guide to morality.

*cf. the Diary of John Evelyn (November 1644): 'Cavaliero Bernini A Florentine Sculptor, Architect, Painter & Poet: who a little before my Comming to the Citty, gave a Publique Opera (for so they call those Shews of that kind) where in he painted the Seanes, cut the Statues, invented the Engines, composed the Musique, writ the Comedy & built the Theater all himselfe.'

If we read Racine's severe strictures on the functions of theatre in the preface to his drama *Phèdre*:

What I can affirm is that in no other play of mine is virtue given greater prominence. The slightest transgressions are severely punished. . . . The passions are portrayed merely in order to show the aberrations to which they give rise; and vice is painted throughout in colours which bring out its hideousness and hatefulness. This is really the objective which everyone working for the theatre should have in mind.[3]

we can see what the more classically minded librettists of the age had at the back of their minds. The more important their message, the less reason why elaborate and fanciful music should be allowed to obscure it. Many of them were happy to assume that they had an important didactic and social role to play; and this attitude led some either to refuse to admit, or else to regret, that opera was a separate genre from spoken drama, over which they had more personal control. The greatest of those who came satisfactorily to terms with the fact that their librettos were for musical setting nevertheless wished their texts to be regarded first and foremost as good literature and felt happy to see critics compare their work with the plays of Corneille and Racine.

The danger was that neo-classical principles could be watered down to justify in opera any social, political or religious theme that was considered suitable. In an age of absolutism the idea of moral virtue could easily become associated with the glorification of the monarch or of the state. Principles, too, clashed with the desire for operas with simple entertainment value, and occasionally absurd explanations had to be given to justify a frivolous libretto. We could take, for example, *La catena d'Adone*, an opera with music by Domenico Mazzocchi performed in papal Rome in 1626, the theme of which was the steadfast love of the shepherd Adonis for the goddess Venus in spite of attempts by a witch Falsirena to abduct him and secure his affections. At the end of the score is an explanation that this apparently hedonistic story is in fact a religious allegory: that Falsirena is a 'soul advised by reason but persuaded by concupiscence' and Adonis 'the man who falls into many errors when apart from God'. We are then informed that 'just as Venus returns to liberate him from every distress and bring him to happiness, so God returns to us with His powerful help, rescues many from earthly harm and gives them a share in heavenly pleasures'.

Such a statement was clearly intended to be taken at its face value, though no one looking at the opera now would have much inkling of religious connotations.

Furthermore, librettists had to come to terms with the fact that musical setting cloaked the poetic fantasy of a text. Some of them felt it was not worth while putting their heart and soul into dramatic poetry when its intrinsic value was totally obscured by music, and one or two Italian librettists of the mid-seventeenth century almost went so far as to say this in their libretto prefaces. Music, unfortunately, has no respect for the literary quality of words; magnificent poetry like the section of the twelfth canto of Tasso's *Gerusaleme liberata* set by Monteverdi as *Il combattimento di Tancredi e Clorinda* stood no more chance of retaining its original effect than poetry by a less gifted writer. Music was far too abstract an art to concern itself with such features at all. It could indulge in 'word painting', and especially in imitating the emotions expressed by the librettist, yet it could never properly recreate the spirit of literature or of any other art.

Intellectual lines of attack on the position of music in opera varied from time to time and from place to place. In most instances music was declared to have usurped its correct function by becoming too prominent and an end in itself. St Evremond, a strong critic of late seventeenth-century opera, expressed the theoretical point of view thus:

Il faut que la Musique soit faite pour les Vers, bien plus que les Vers pour la Musique; c'est au Musicien à suivre l'ordre du Poète....[4]

Occasionally, too, it was thought necessary to drag up the old, Aristotelian concept that music was an 'imitative' art and should therefore imitate the words.[5] The whole intellectual standpoint was based on the pure accident that, since the poet wrote his words first, the musician had to follow his lead. Algarotti in his *Essay* went so far as to say that the poet was the one who should 'carry in his mind a comprehensive view of the *whole* of the drama'.[6] This meant nothing less than that the other artists should obey his general directives.

Gluck claimed in the score of his opera *Alceste*, 1767, to have restricted music 'to its true office of serving poetry by means of expression and by following the situation of the story'.[7] Algarotti's *Essay* may well have been one of the decisive influences prompting him to 'restrict' his art in this manner, though his statement in no way contradicts the fact that *Alceste* is good primarily because its music is so. While Gluck may have attempted to restore to Italian opera of his time dramatic cohesion and make music 'serve' poetry, he did not let his music be totally subservient to the text he was given.

In any case the only way in which music could properly have been made the servant of the text would have been to put the clock back to the period of the very first operas. In these there was a serious attempt to tone down the lyrical qualities that music possesses and by and large to keep it tied stylistically to a close imitation of speech. Musical lyricism could not be contained for long, however, and in no time at all short arias and ensembles were beginning to proliferate in operatic scores. Music now, so to speak, had its head, and all chances of making it properly subservient to anything else were gone for ever. All that librettists could effectively ask for in future was a compromise between their demands and those of the musicians. Such compromises, when made on later occasions for the sake of better music drama, were a positive step towards the creation of operatic works of art.

1   F. Algarotti, *Essay on the opera*, English edn, Glasgow, 1768, pp. 5–6.

2   *The letters of Mozart and his family*, ed. Anderson, London, 1938, ii, 977 ff.

3   *Phaedra and other plays*, Penguin edn, 1963, pp. 146–7.

4   St Evremond, *Oeuvres meslées*, London, 1705, ii, 105.

5   cf. S. Arteaga, *Le rivoluzioni del teatro musicale italiano*, 2nd edn, Venice, 1785, ii, 308.

6   Algarotti, op. cit., p. 15.

7   O. Strunk, *Source readings in music history*, London, 1952, p. 674.

2

OPERA IN THE AGE OF ABSOLUTISM

The team of artistic enthusiasts, called the *Camerata*, that met at the houses of Count Bardi and later of Jacopo Corsi in Florence in the late sixteenth century has become famous for its experiments in dramatic music that eventually led to the production of the first opera, *Dafne*, in 1597. The group had a fluctuating and varied membership including high-ranking amateurs, intellectuals and professional artists. Of the many who took part the names of a few have come down to us, particularly important being Ottavio Rinuccini, the poet, and Emilio de'Cavalieri, Jacopo Peri, Giulio Caccini and Marco da Gagliano, all musicians. These were all in one way or another employed by the then Grand Duke of Tuscany, Ferdinand I (reigning 1587–1609), and it was natural that he and other members of the ruling Medici family should be interested in the experiments. Gagliano records that 'Giovanni Medici and other illustrious gentlemen of our city' watched the production of *Dafne*,[1] and further signs of approval from above were the performances of two new operas—*Euridice*, with music largely by Peri, and *Il rapimento di Cefalo*, with music largely by Caccini—in Florence in 1600 as part of the festivities honouring the marriage of King Henry IV of France and Maria Medici, Ferdinand's daughter.

Thus, opera had no sooner made its first appearance than it became a court activity, a fact which should surprise no one aware of the social and political conditions of the period. The family dynasties that wielded political power in most European states also maintained close control over the arts. During the seventeenth and

eighteenth centuries the degree and manner of autocratic supervision affected the quality of opera and largely determined the
amount of operatic patronage in other, non-court circles. The
looser this supervision, the more opportunities there were for
others to support it on their own initiative. But whether court
control was direct or indirect, its tastes and opinions infiltrated
everywhere. Its own opera, too, had a glamour which attracted
the attention of all to the art.

The attachment of opera to court ceremonial had a fairly immediate effect upon its shape and future development. So long as it
remained a purely private affair in a court environment it was
usually an occasional work performed perhaps on one night only.
Often it was among the plays, masquerades and other theatrical
extravaganza ordered to celebrate a royal wedding, visit or birth-
day. The pattern of festivities to honour such events had been set
in Renaissance times by Italian princes and rapidly imitated in
France and elsewhere. The reigning prince invited his chief guests
and aristocracy to court, and then entertained them with hunts and
tourneys in the daytime, with theatricals and banquets at suitable
hours, and with balls in the evening. This was the pattern when the
Princess Margherita of Savoy arrived in Mantua in 1608 to marry
Prince Francesco Gonzaga.[2] An opera, *Arianna*, with text by
Rinuccini and music by Monteverdi, formed part of the festivities
and was performed on the fifth evening in a new, specially built
theatre. On other evenings there were plays and ballets including
Il ballo delle ingrate with music again by Monteverdi, later published
in his eighth madrigal book; and one night was set aside for a
magnificent 'Siege of a castle upon an artificial island in a lake'.
This last-mentioned was a rehearsed battle spectacle between two
opposing armies, one representing the Christians and the other the
Turks, ending naturally with the defeat of the latter, the annihilation
of their ships and the blowing up of their castle in a fine fireworks
display. The Mantuan musicians were very much concerned with all
these entertainments, since music was required not only in the opera
and ballets but also in the *intermedii*, or entr'actes, to Guarini's play,
Idropica, and also in the 'Siege'. The 'Siege' started with the appearance on the lake of a *carro trionfale*, water-borne and miracul-
ously drawn across to where the court was stationed, carrying a lady
who sang the role of 'Fortune' and thirteen instrumentalists who
accompanied her.

Like other branches of theatre, opera could be performed out of doors as well as in. The most famous of all outdoor operas, *Costanza e fortezza*, with music by Johann Fux, was performed in a specially constructed open-air theatre at Prague in 1723 to celebrate the coronation of the Emperor Charles VI. Such open-air theatres were often the best solution to the problem of accommodating large audiences. Their chief disadvantage was lack of protection from the weather, a fact pointed out by Lady Mary Wortley Montagu when she visited Vienna in 1716 and saw a production of Fux's *Angelica* in the garden of the Favorita. After describing the great size of the theatre and the skill shown in the stage designs and the 'great variety of machines', she went on:

... the ladies all sitting in the open air, exposes them to great inconveniences, for there is but one canopy for the imperial family; and the first night it was represented, a shower of rain happening, the opera was broken off, and the company crowded away in such confusion, I was almost squeezed to death.[3]

Yet for at least a section of the male aristocracy present, a shower of rain was no more unfortunate during an opera than during one of the many hunts or tourneys arranged on other days of the festival. An opera was certainly no more important than other events. The prince gave those guests with sportsmenlike propensities, or with the desire to act in pageants and parades, as much of a programme as he gave those interested in the fine arts. Opera on these occasions was part of a bigger ceremonial—one of a number of events and not an affair in isolation. It was a spectacle equalling but perhaps not surpassing a ball or stag hunt.[4]

The many events comprising a court festival may collectively be considered as an allegory acted by the princes, aristocracy and their attendant professionals—poets, musicians, courtiers, pages and others—to emphasise the unity of the court and the lasting ascendency of the ruling house. The motive was even more deeply political than the official reason given for the composite collection of events. The basic aim was often to assemble the aristocracy round the person of the sovereign—this was particularly the case with Louis XIV's fêtes at Versailles—and to associate them with his policies by making them take part in the various activities. The motive was sufficient to excuse, in the eyes of people at court, the gigantic expense involved.

The part that opera could play on such occasions, and in the more general everyday life of the court, obviously varied according to time and place. It did not at first become an automatic favourite with the courts that keenly patronised the arts, and there was probably a simple reason why. Opera, even in its early years, had to be highly professionally performed by trained singers to be effective, a fact barring most court amateurs from taking part. Many courtiers in the seventeenth as well as the sixteenth century liked to show their skill at miming and dancing, and therefore preferred various forms of ballet and masquerade in which they themselves could take a prominent role.

Particular attention should be paid to the most sophisticated of these entertainments in which the courtier himself could shine: the late sixteenth- and early seventeenth-century French *ballet de cour*, to which the English masque was related. The various subdivisions, or *entrées*, of a ballet could be more or less connected with a central theme, and allowed for the appearance of both professional actors and amateurs—the latter of course being the persons of high birth whose entries were the centre of interest. The climax was in most cases the final dance in which actors of high rank moved on to the floor of the room to dance with selected ladies of the audience. The various *entrées* with their action and song were therefore a preliminary to a general dance. The ballet as a whole had to be acted either on the same level as the floor of the room or, if on a raised stage or platform, connected to the floor by means of a ramp. There was no absolute division, as there was later in an opera house, between stage and auditorium.

French influence in Italy, especially in Florence, at the beginning of the seventeenth century meant the increased popularity of the French-style ballet at Italian courts, so that Italian composers were at first put to work more often on ballets than on operas. It is significant that Ottavio Rinuccini and Giulio Caccini were invited to Paris in the early years of the century and came home fully aware of French court art. Good examples of how the French ballet form could be adapted to Italian taste can be seen in Monteverdi's already mentioned *Il ballo delle ingrate*, and in Francesca Caccini's *La liberazione di Ruggiero*, 1625. Both works begin like operas but lead to dancing sequences, while the second terminates with a *ballo a cavallo* or musical ride.

The appearance of opera was bound to hasten the development

of ballets with dramatic coherence and with through-composed music. The Italian ballets mentioned contain all the recognisable musical techniques, notably the monodic recitative, of contemporary opera. In the first decades of the century there was a move in France also towards ballet set throughout to music, though the parallel with Italian procedures stops when we consider the vocal styles adopted and the lack of a proper French equivalent to Italian recitative. De Luynes, favourite of Louis XIII, may himself have sung the title role in *La délivrance de Renaud*, a ballet acted at the French court in 1617.[5] This was less usual than the appearance of high-ranking members of court as dancers. But in all these cases the entry of persons of the highest rank fundamentally affected the function and atmosphere of ballet, which was ultimately a form as much for the actors as for the spectators.

Although it is not impossible to find mention of aristocratic performers in the earliest operas, most of these works were addressed by professionals to the court. If opera then was to become popular in such high circles, it had to have sufficiently attractive qualities of its own to make even those rulers and courtiers with a flair for dancing and acting just sit back and enjoy it. The fact that they gradually patronised it in more and more European courts is proof of its attractions. Reasons for the growth of its popularity were many, though we should perhaps single out especially the fine staging and singing, both of which the Italians excelled at and which helped the Italian operatic forms to spread abroad.

Fine stagecraft had previously been a feature of the *intermedii*, or entr'actes, in sixteenth-century court plays. The allegorical figures, the furies, deities, dragons and monsters, the scenes of paradise and of the *inferno*, all of which had been popular in *intermedii*, were part of that totally unreal and fantastic theatrical world that appealed to high-class audiences and therefore quickly passed over into many of the early operas which were court patronised. Note one of the magnificent stage effects in *Il rapimento di Cefalo* of 1600:

What filled everyone with absolute amazement was that the cloud, several layers thick, moved forward enlarging and contracting itself in a natural manner, and was seen perpetually to take different shapes, at one moment that of a dolphin or horse, at another that of a wood or mountain or some indistinct object. Then, as the rim of that cloud machine passed behind other clouds, the scenery changed and a mighty ocean appeared where previously woods and land had been . . . The white-crested waves rippled and purled as they turned over and under. Further miraculous qualities of that most delightful scene were gradually revealed, to the delight of those watching. For from a corner a sea monster, or rather huge whale, fourteen yards in circumference, was unexpectedly seen to rise from a great depth, as though heaving and straining to reach the surface. And from the other side a chariot appeared, a machine not unequal to the whale in size, drawn by four horses. At first these horses were barely visible, with just their wet heads above the water, but climbing and furiously pounding their hooves, they gradually materialised. They panted foaming at the mouth, shook their manes, and pressed irresistibly forward. Their driver was a resplendent charioteer skilfully and graciously poised. His chariot was exquisitely made and shone with gold and jewels, like the reins of the horses. This sumptuousness was necessary to give a proper impression of the chariot, that of the Sun.[6]

This then was the sort of spectacle that court audiences admired. The lavishness and skill of this production must have put the contemporary *Euridice* with Peri's music, a much simpler yet more famous opera in musical history, in the shade. M. A. Buonarroti, who made the description of the scenery recorded above, called *Il rapimento* 'the biggest of its type that had ever been seen or heard' and declared that more than one hundred musicians were engaged in it.

Opera benefited from the coincidence that it began at a time when Italian stage designers were fast improving their techniques and were able to produce the stupendous effects mentioned. Of their many new or relatively new devices, the proscenium arch was particularly important, allowing the spectator to view the stage from a much narrower angle than hitherto and consequently increasing the designers' opportunity to make spectacular illusion seem real. Quick changes of scenery were made easy by installing painted sets of flaps in the wings. These flaps, running parallel to the front of the stage, could be drawn from either side to meet in the middle of the stage and then drawn back to let another pair of flaps, and scene, appear.[7] The arch had further uses. It hid the elaborate apparatus controlling the flying machines and allowed designers to produce a better illusion of perspective. Most seventeenth- and early eighteenth-century stage designs for operas show quite clearly the side façades narrowing towards some central vanishing point.

The fact that opera began in a part of Europe where the art of stagecraft had been developed to its highest degree was therefore significant. It helps to explain the extraordinary spread of Italian opera over most of Europe in the seventeenth and eighteenth centuries. Even in France, where the court had reservations about Italian opera when Cardinal Mazarin attempted to introduce it in the 1640's and 50's, the art of the stage designer and engineer Giacomo Torelli was generally received with acclamation.[8] In England, the reception of Inigo Jones, who applied Italian stage techniques to productions of Jacobean court masques, was similarly favourable. Stage designers were therefore very much responsible for strengthening the Italian cultural image.

If expert stagecraft was one thing at which the Italians excelled, expert singing was another. The spread of opera was in no small part due to the extraordinary ability of *castrati* and *prime donne* to entrance all who heard them. Just as the engagement of a composer was sometimes a matter of diplomatic activity and correspondence between rulers, so an intense rivalry began between interested courts for the best singers. The fees they were able to demand rose astronomically and increased the burden of debt incurred by those many petty European rulers who sought after a magnificent opera company to enhance their international prestige.

The extension of opera from Florence, Rome, Mantua and other towns where it was first performed was very much a matter of personal influence. Outside Italy the people most likely to patronise it at first were Italian princesses married to members of foreign royal houses, papal nuncios and other envoys from Italy, or the occasional Italian like Mazarin who became a foreign citizen and achieved great political power in his country of adoption. Alternatively, foreign royalty and envoys visiting Italy, especially Venice, for the Carnival season may have seen opera there and been sufficiently impressed to wish to promote it at home. The first opera performance outside Italy seems to have taken place at Salzburg in 1618 and thereafter other states and cities undertook similar projects.

The methods adopted by those introducing opera to any court usually followed a recognisable procedure. A few selected opera artists were called for, and an opera was given in a temporary theatre or room in the palace. If this proved successful, attempts were then made to put the operatic troupe on a permanent basis.

Where possible its members were absorbed into the existing musical organisation of the royal household, and in a number of cases there began a virtual take-over of the royal chapel by operatic musicians. The final flourish was the building of a large theatre, and a gala opening. In the earlier days of opera, when Italians were the sole experts, it was inevitable that the core of the opera company should be Italian. What is interesting is that in so many cases court opera remained an Italian art sung in that language. Some of the reasons why Italians exercised such a masterly hold have already been suggested. Another was the ease with which a princeling could always engage Italian companies and artists. This saved many autocrats the trouble of having slowly and painfully to build companies with local talent.

The question of which language opera was to be sung in occurs here for the first and not the last time. Italian opera abroad was not for many years associated with any 'popular' movement, primarily because it was too expensive, because its subject matter was not geared to the taste of the populace, and because its language was not one understood by the majority. It was really an alien, exotic entertainment hardly touching the lives of the ordinary people. Those at court who did not understand Italian probably considered the singing sufficiently superior to compensate for the incomprehensibility of the text. In any case, translations of librettos were easily obtainable. Many courts did not consider Italian a foreign language at all since some were allied to Italian states by marriage or, like Austria and Spain, held Italian territorial possessions. Italian was spoken freely, for instance, in Viennese salons and literary academies, while the imperial family too was quite fluent. Vienna attracted many of the best Italian librettists into residence, and no Italian court could claim like the Austrian that such famous poets as Nicolò Minato, Silvio Stampiglia, Apostolo Zeno and Pietro Metastasio had all at one time or another been in its employ.

One important result of all this was the growth of a tradition that opera well sung was opera in Italian. It may have been true that Italy was the chief arsenal of singers, yet the rest of Europe was not devoid of talent. Foreign singers, however, who wished for the same success as Italians and, equally important, wished to be paid on the same scale, usually had to enter the world of court opera, which in most countries had Italian words. The tradition was in its turn hard to break, since most seventeenth- and eighteenth-century foreign rulers felt no great need to patronise opera sung in the vernacular. Powerful additional arguments in favour of the *status quo* were that Italian was a more 'musical' language and therefore more suitable, also that *castrati* and *prime donne* sang best in their own tongue. It should be remembered that when Handel made Italian singers perform *Esther* in English, their pronunciation caused derisive comment.[9]

France is the outstanding exception to the rule that Italian opera gained complete ascendancy in European courts. Mazarin's attempt to introduce Italian opera to the court there followed the usual procedure already described, and was finally crowned by the erection of a magnificent if impractical theatre in the Tuileries. This should have been ready in 1660 to coincide with the marriage of Louis XIV to the Infanta Maria Theresa of Spain but was not completed until 1662. Determining factors in Mazarin's policy seem to have been a genuine personal love of opera, which he had seen in his youth in Rome, and the political consideration of keeping the court entertained. His ultimate failure was due to the unpopularity of his fiscal measures to pay for these operas and other extravagances, and to the conflict of taste once the young king Louis XIV, who preferred ballet to Italian opera, began to have a say in what the court should perform. The French had, since the introduction of the first Italian operas, interspersed them with ballet *entrées*. In the 1650's these grew in size and importance, since the young king danced in them himself and with him members of the court. The dancers even included the exiled Duke of York, later James II of England.[10] This galaxy of rank and perhaps talent naturally drew all attention to the dances leaving the operas largely without support. The last in the line of Italian operas, *Ercole amante*,[11] was performed in 1662 to open the Tuileries theatre and was judged a comparative failure like its immediate predecessors.

This, however, was not the end of opera patronage by the French court, for where opera in Italian had failed, opera in French was eventually to succeed. The next step in the story was the attempt by certain individuals, notably the poet Pierre Perrin, to establish in France a new form of opera in the vernacular. Louis XIV himself seems to have made no effort to encourage opera in any language, but since opera already existed in other states, and since there was pressure to promote it again in France, he decided that it should be brought firmly under royal control in conformity with his policy of extending the power of central government in every direction. One of the most striking phrases in his patent to the composer Jean-Baptiste Lully in 1672, giving him sole right to promote opera in France, was the following: 'Les Sciences et les Arts étant les ornemens les plus considérables des Etats.'[12] The arts were a state business, and opera therefore had to become a state monopoly.

The desire to turn opera into part of the state propaganda machine was one reason behind the granting of this patent. The arts had to buttress up the state citadel, as we can see in Lully's opera prologues which present a flattering allegory of Louis himself. Similar propaganda found its way by one means or another into most court operas of the age of absolutism. A preamble in the libretto of Lully's opera *Cadmus et Hermione*, 1673, explained what was to be shown in the prologue in this case:

Le sens allegorique de ce sujet est si clair, qu'il est inutile de l'expliquer. Il suffit de dire que LE ROY s'est mis au dessus des louanges ordinaires, & que pour former quelque idée de la grandeur & de l'éclat de sa gloire, il a fallu s'élever jusqu'à la Divinité même de la lumière, qui est le corps de sa Devise.

Thus the prologue was intended to equate the Sun with Louis, already known as *Le Roi Soleil* since the time of an earlier court ballet in which he had appeared as a personification of the Sun. The job of the librettist, Philippe Quinault, was therefore to choose one of the Apollo myths most suitable for the occasion. The subject of the God killing the Python had already been used by Rinuccini in the first opera *Dafne* and seemed the obvious one to use again. Calling his prologue *Le Serpent Python*, Quinault set about his simple allegory. It begins with songs and dances by pastoral characters honouring the Sun God, but the festivities are interrupted by Envy, who causes confusion by summoning from the nearby swamp a hideous monster

jettant de flammes par la gueule & par les yeux, qui forment la seule lumière qui éclaire le Théatre.

Envy's glory, however, is shortlived, for suddenly

des traits enflâmez percent l'épaisseur des nuages, & fondent sur le SERPENT.

She flees, and Apollo in all his majesty appears to receive the praise

of his worshippers. The monster from the swamp was a reference
to the then French military campaign in the Low Countries, and
Apollo's victory a specific allusion to Louis' triumphs in war and a
general apotheosis of kingship.

   The official start of opera in French was the patent afforded the
librettist and poet Perrin in June 1669 by Louis, entitling him to
form an *Académie d'opéra* and stating that for a period of twelve
years no one else was permitted to produce operas or 'représenta-
tions en Musique en Vers François' in the French realm.[13] This
Académie was a purely commercial venture and not one that Louis
himself seems to have patronised. Perrin's difficulty, once his
monopoly was established, was to get an operatic company into
being and keep it active, since his own funds were slender. His
basic failure was in borrowing the finances from persons who
quarrelled with him over artistic policy and tried to control his
venture by having him thrown into prison for debt. At this moment
he did the only thing open to him, and sold his patent to Lully,
then Louis' *Surintendant de la Musique de la Chambre*, who offered to
pay for it. There can be no question of Lully having behaved dis-
honestly over this transaction, as has sometimes been suggested.
The new patent, signed by Louis in March 1672, granted to Lully
and his descendents a perpetual monopoly of opera in any language
in France. The new privilege was thus far wider than the old.
Partly because the two men were on very good personal terms,
Louis took much greater interest in Lully's venture than he had in
Perrin's. Allowing Lully to call his company the *Académie royale de
musique*, the king was personally consulted over the scenarios of
new operas and involved himself in other details. However, he
rarely travelled to Paris to see a new production in the public
theatre. Usually he required the *Académie* to bring it to him. In
royal command performances at Versailles or St Germain musicians
in Louis' private household often took part side by side with
members of Lully's Parisian company. On the Parisian stage the
fact that an opera had been seen by the king and approved of was
an important factor in its success. It was essential, too, that it
should be, since Louis gave no regular financial support for the
Académie's public performances any more than he had financially
supported Perrin. The concession in both Perrin's and Lully's
patents that all comers to the public theatre were to be charged for
admission—courtiers had been accustomed to claim free admission

to theatres—certainly contributed ultimately to the stability of Lully's finances. Nevertheless Lully had to rely on 'popular' support to a degree no composer writing merely for private court performances ever had to do. This gives the lie to any suggestion that Lully's heroic operas were aimed solely at pleasing the monarch, although Louis' support was essential and his taste reflected in the final artistic result.

Court opera did not therefore necessarily have to remain a purely private affair run by the ruler at his own expense, but could be put on a semi- or totally commercial basis with partial or nominal royal patronage. Louis' method was a convenient one for any monarch living outside the chief city of his realm. A king like Charles III of Naples, who spent periods of the year in his capital city, could build a royal theatre conveniently next to his palace yet also close to the centre of city life. Opened in 1737, Charles' S. Carlo theatre ran regular 'seasons' which the rulers and aristocracy regularly patronised. In several countries regular attendance at the opera became for members of the richer classes a normal part of their social life. The important fact is that such attendance enabled rulers like Charles III to open their theatres to a high-class, paying audience whose taste was in line with the court's and whose aim was therefore to preserve something of the atmosphere of a court opera. Since, however, such opera was expensive, and in some countries not in the vernacular, it could be run commercially only where there was a large élite class interested in bolstering up its snob value. The smaller the state, the more the enthusiastic prince had to foot the bill himself, if his opera was to be of international standing.

While autocrats were lavish in their support of the arts, they were also notorious for their changes of artistic policy. Opera was completely at the mercy of the rulers' capricious whim and could be struck down at the least hint of political disturbances or of economic stringency. In some states it suffered from the excessive lavishness with which rulers supported it. Take the example of Duke Charles Eugene of Württemberg who, it has been estimated, spent in the early 1760's some 300,000 gulden per year—that was a third of his own income and one tenth of the entire revenue of the state[14]—on his theatres alone. No wonder that Charles Burney wrote: 'The Duke of Württemberg has been accused of indulging his passion for music to such excess as to ruin both his country and

people.'[15] Opera together with other extravagant court entertainments was, alas, far too often a concomitant of bad government,
of an empty exchequer, of a total disregard for the welfare of the
subjects of the realm. Prodigious expenditure of this kind could not
continue for ever and was bound one day to bring a reaction.
Burney, visiting the Duke's residence of Ludwigsburg in 1772,
found the music there a pale shadow of what it had been only a
decade previously. Since then Jommelli, the composer, Noverre,
the ballet master, and others who had contributed to the outstanding artistic successes of the Württemberg opera, had been
dismissed and the theatre now stood empty, a monument to past
memories.

There is no doubt that a change of taste, too, could adversely
affect the fortunes of opera. Numerous were the occasions when the
accession of a new ruler meant the dismissal of musicians of the
chapel and opera, not just because of the expense involved but
because he preferred to spend his money on something else. Few
states had a ruling dynasty whose leading members were consistent
patrons of music. The Austrian Hapsburg line produced a succession
of such men, the Emperors Ferdinand III, Leopold I, Joseph I and
Charles VI, whose rule in turn covered the period 1637–1740, all
being proficient musicians and even composers.[16] Once opera had
been established on a permanent footing following the accession of
Leopold in 1658, it was not subject to so many of the violent ups
and downs of opera in smaller and less affluent countries. With
music an essential part of the training of young princes and
princesses, the imperial family itself performed in private cantata
and even opera productions. The opera Euristeo with music by
Antonio Caldara, 1724, has its place in history because the cast and
orchestra were allegedly comprised solely of high-ranking members
of the court, the dances executed by archduchesses, and the keyboard
continuo part realised by the Emperor Charles himself.[17]

So far we have mentioned only opera produced in ruling court
circles. Opera of the court type could also be patronised by members
of the aristocracy on their own estates. Whether they did this with
any consistency depended on their private finances and to a large
extent on governmental policy. For example, the Empress Maria
Theresa of Austria, who succeeded Charles VI on the throne in
1740, encouraged powerful Austro-Hungarian nobles to arrange
festivals similar to those at court in Vienna. Her aim was to make

them imitate the pleasures of the central court and so ignore Hungarian separatist movements that might have dangerous political repercussions. Joseph Haydn was one of several composers engaged by princely patrons to write operas for festivals of this kind.[18] There was little to distinguish one such ceremony from another. 'It would weary my readers', wrote the composer Karl von Dittersdorf about the visit of the Emperor Francis I to Schlosshof, the seat of Prince Friedrich von Hildburghausen in 1754, 'were I to make a long yarn about all the many fêtes, fireworks, Bacchanal scenes, and hunting-parties which were the order of the day.'[19]

The place however with the most renowned private patrons was undoubtedly Rome. Several high-ranking prelates resident there in the seventeenth century and first decades of the eighteenth—the Cardinals Alessandro di Montalto, Antonio Barberini, and Pietro Ottoboni, for instance—were prominent opera enthusiasts, as was Queen Christina of Sweden who retired to Rome in 1655 following her abdication and conversion to the Roman Catholic faith. The Roman religious seminaries were also important, especially for their interest at the beginning of the seventeenth century in opera with a religious or 'moral' content. The increasing vogue for purely secular opera forced the Popes on more than one occasion to wonder whether such an art, with its opulence, its sensuousness, its singing stars with their allegedly loose morals, could be permitted. Some of them made little or no objection, and one, Clement IX (1667–9), had himself been a librettist of some distinction. Pope Innocent XI (1676–89), on the other hand, took a severer line, reviving in a sharper form a sixteenth-century edict against the appearance of women on the theatrical stage, and in the year of his death forbidding opera performances altogether. Pope Clement XI (1700–21) also imposed this latter ban during the first years of his pontificate. The prohibition of women on the stage affected Roman opera for many years. For a large part of the eighteenth century feminine roles were taken by *castrati*.

The nobility had a decisive influence over the course of opera in eighteenth-century England where the monarchy, shorn of much of its power in Commonwealth and Restoration times, could hardly gratify its artistic tastes to any scandalous extent. Neither were members of the English aristocracy tempted to patronise opera on the grand Continental scale. The first Duke of Chandos is the one who seems to have behaved closest to the foreign model, keeping a large musical establishment at his palace at Cannons (built 1719)[20] and becoming famous for his patronage of Handel. The nobility as a group came into its own once opera, which had been known in England before, was put in 1705 on a regular 'seasonal' basis. It now quickly became an Italianate form, sung in Italian and set usually by Continental composers. Royal patronage, keen though it was in the case of both George I and George II, was not the decisive factor here that it would have been in other countries. Squabbles between members of the Hanoverian royal family, and the fact that they were of German origin and therefore 'foreigners' in an English world, comparatively decreased their power to control artistic taste. The king's presence in the theatre to hear, for example, an opera by Handel was no guarantee that the house would be full and supported by the majority of rich Londoners. In fact, Italian opera in London really required the separate patronage of both royalty and society. Associations like the *Royal Academy of Music*, 1719–28, and the *Opera of the Nobility*, 1733–7, with their lists of royal and private subscribers, were founded to keep it alive. There was nothing preventing the foundation of rival associations either—with the royal family divided in its support—all of which enlivened debate and acrimony between various factions.

The ultimate financial failure of all these groups in the heyday of Italian opera in London, which we might say covered the period 1710–40 approximately, was caused by precisely the same sort of reason that caused its collapse in other places: the prodigiously high cost of production and the enthusiastic patronage of only a small fraction of the populace. Sufficient support was always forthcoming for a new company to be founded on the ruins of the old, and in fact Italian opera in London continued well into the nineteenth century. Yet firmer support from a larger class might have been in evidence had composers of genius like Handel seriously turned their attention to opera in English with scenarios more closely suited to local taste. The fine dramatic qualities of Handel's oratorios in English show that he was quite capable of writing English opera if he chose. Yet his actions seem to have been bedevilled by the belief that fashionable opera should be in Italian, and he never followed the plea of Aaron Hill and other nationalists to write opera in the English language.[21]

The degree of strict autocratic supervision of opera had a great deal to do with the way audiences behaved in court theatres. Unruly acclamation, clapping, signs of disapproval, would have been quite out of the question in the theatre of some opera-loving autocrat like Frederick the Great of Prussia, whose accustomed position was the front of the pit, from where he could keep a sharp watch on the orchestra and on the musical score through his opera glasses.[22] A monarch like Charles III of Naples, on the other hand, who attended the opera more out of habit than out of love and who was recorded on one occasion as having talked through one half of a performance and slept through the other,[23] was bound to communicate his attitude to others with, we suspect, some relaxation in their behaviour. In Hanoverian England where etiquette was less rigid still, riots and unruly demonstrations could take place in a theatre even when members of the royal family were present. Therefore, the rumbustiousness of the audience could be in inverse proportion to the strictness of the protocol. This, however, was not the only rule determining social manners. Seventeenth- and eighteenth-century audiences were far more noisy than audiences nowadays, and we should not in every case confuse reports of noise in old theatres with reports of downright unruliness. Noise and manners form part of one subject discussed in the next chapter.

1 A. Solerti, *Gli albori del melodramma*, Milan, 1904, ii, 68.

2 F. Follino, *Compendio delle sontuose feste fatte l'anno MDCVIII nella città di Mantova, per le reali nozze del Serenissimo Prencipe D. Francesco Gonzaga, con la Serenissima Infante Margherita di Savoia*, Mantua, 1608.

3 Lady Mary Wortley Montagu, *The letters and works*, ed. Wharncliffe, London, 1893, i, 238.

4 cf. G. Tzschimmer, *Die Durchlauchtigste Zusammenkunfft oder historische Erzehlung, was . . . Johann George der Ander, Herzog zu Sachsen . . . auffuhren und vorstellen lassen*, Nurnberg, 1680.

5 H. Prunières, *Le ballet de cour en France*, Paris, 1914, p. 116.

6 Solerti, op. cit., iii, 17–18.

7 cf. S. Towneley Worsthorne, *Venetian opera in the seventeenth century*, Oxford, 1954, pp. 18 ff.

8 H. Prunières, *L'opéra italien en France avant Lulli*, Paris, 1913, pp. 68 ff.

9 O. E. Deutsch, *Handel, a documentary biography*, London, 1955, p. 301.

10 J. Howell, *The nuptialls of Peleus and Thetis* (translation and comments upon), London, 1654, pp. 7–8.

11 Prunières, *L'opéra italien*, pp. 282 ff.

12 Text of Lully's patent in N. Demuth, *French opera: its development to the Revolution*, Artemis, Sussex, 1963, pp. 282–3.

13 Text of Perrin's patent in Demuth, op. cit., pp. 268–9.

14 A. Yorke-Long, *Music at court*, London, 1954, p. 61.

15 *Dr Burney's musical tours in Europe*, ed. Scholes, London, 1959, ii, 36.

16 G. Adler, 'Die Kaiser Ferdinand III, Leopold I, Joseph I und Karl VI als Tonsetzer und Förderer der Musik', *Vierteljahrsschrift für Musikwissenschaft* viii (1892), 252 ff.

17 ibid., pp. 259 and 272.

18 cf. M. Horányi, *The magnificence of Eszterháza*, English edn, London, 1962, pp. 62 ff.

19 K. von Dittersdorf, *The autobiography*, English edn, London, 1896, p. 64.

20 cf. D. Defoe, *A tour through England and Wales*, vol II, letter 3 (a description of part of Middlesex).

21 Deutsch, op. cit., p. 299.

22 *Dr Burney's musical tours*, ii, 164 and 207.

23 C. de Brosses, *Lettres familières écrites d'Italie en 1739 et 1740*, Paris, 1858, i, 383.

3

OPERA FOR THE POPULACE

Of immeasurable importance to the development of early opera was its increasing popularity with the general public. In Italy, France and other major West European countries opera was by the mid-eighteenth century far from being a reserved entertainment for a ruling and privileged class. Naturally the quality and form of opera varied according to its function and to the taste of the audience. Many comic operas designed to please the bourgeoisie were the clear antithesis of works at contemporary courts. Yet there is danger in supposing that 'court' and 'popular' operas were always different. Audiences often overlapped, and tastes were to some extent similar. Lully's operas, for example, appealed to a wide stratum of society. In addition, artists were often engaged almost simultaneously on works for court and bourgeois audiences, and sometimes found it difficult or else unnecessary to change their style and methods.

Popular patronage began with the rise of commercial opera houses, and the emergence of the first of these, at Venice in 1637,[1] was therefore an important historical event. Particular attention should be paid to operatic practices at Venice since these were later copied in a host of court and commercial theatres in other parts of Europe. When a city exerts such influence over the development of opera as Venice did in its seventeenth-century heyday, and as Naples did in the 1720's and following decades, reasons for its supremacy are usually: the quality of its productions, the international gathering among its audiences, and the subsequent artistic influence on opera elsewhere. In the case of the Venetian Republic the quality of productions was determined by several factors. Venetian musicians, especially those of St Mark's, had achieved international fame since the middle of the sixteenth century and continued to attract foreign musicians to come and study under them. The city therefore had an excellent musical tradition. It had the necessary wealth and, equally important, no autocratic interference. In addition, it enjoyed the presence of a rich, international society at certain seasons of which the Carnival between Christmas and Lent was the most popular. These foreigners were the ones to carry the renown and promotion of Venetian opera to other countries.

Venetian nobles provided the backbone of support by building theatres which they then ran commercially under impresarios. The number of such theatres varied from time to time, though up to seven have been recorded as staging opera in one season.[2] Venice therefore believed in competition, and from the first adopted totally different methods from those adopted in France with its monopoly. In fact, competition between opera houses thrived in Venice to a degree unknown elsewhere during the seventeenth and eighteenth centuries.

All these factors were likely to have a cumulative effect on the course of opera itself. In the first place, the wealth of talent attracted to Venice and the large number of good productions gave Venetian audiences an opportunity to discern good from bad and to acquire a connoisseurship of the art. New developments were quickly assessed, and accepted or disapproved. Secondly, the very profusion of good things induced a wish for quick change and for greater sensation. This was the danger of the Venetian commercial system, though the usual alternative of the time—the dictatorial control of one man at court—also had disadvantages. The fickle and fast-changing taste of Venetian audiences was possibly less damaging to the course of opera than too much autocratic domination. Autocratic patronage often resulted in too uncertain or else too rigid a control over artistic policy. Frederick the Great of Prussia was one monarch who knew precisely what he liked and disliked, and who personally supervised the operas of his Berlin theatre in the 1740's and early 50's with a firmness that removed all chance of unauthorised artistic innovation. Musically, the Berlin operas of those years were cast in a similar and rather conservative mould. By comparison opera in the hotly competitive atmosphere of

Venice changed much faster. Artists in such conditions found themselves compelled to move with the times or get ahead of them.

Carnival with its crowded calendar of amusements was the great social event of the Venetian year. It was also the time when masks and fancy costumes were commonly worn in public places; and this habit of moving around incognito had an important effect upon both the general atmosphere of the season and the theatricals performed during it. Carnival was in its own way as theatrically artificial as a court festival. The type of life, however, was different and had its compensations, for princes and aristocrats cramped by the court conventions of their own countries could walk through Venice in disguise and pursue relatively private lives for the duration of the season. The system of masks was found convenient by many other people too. Mozart wrote at a much later period from Verona that masks at the opera were a good thing because he did not have to raise his hat and address anyone else by name.[3] The public's habit of wearing disguise affected the quality of opera and other forms of theatre. Paintings of St Mark's Square during the Venetian Carnival sometimes depict a moment when actors are performing comedies on temporary platforms. Many among the spectators wear masks as do the actors, a fact which seems curiously to unite the two and associate them with the same event. Some such curious link probably obtained inside opera houses; and although the singers may not have worn masks—members of the audience certainly did—it is no mere chance that opera librettos of the great Venetian seventeenth-century period abound in *travestimenti* and disguise of all sorts. Even more important than this, Venetian audiences acquired a certain anonymity, whatever their class, because of the masks they wore. Disguise did not do away with differences of rank between one person and the next, but it did help to give audiences as a whole a superficially united appearance. A further bond uniting people of different classes was the straightforward desire of all to take part in the gaiety of the occasion. Venetian opera was entertainment pure and simple.

The very varied constitution of Venetian audiences must be borne in mind when assessments of Venetian opera are made. The nobility, ambassadors, and others of high rank customarily spent the evening in their boxes, while the gondoliers, tradespeople, and other less affluent classes crowded into the pit. Some theatres at Venice were more luxurious than others, and so attracted a greater proportion of the wealthy. Nevertheless the characteristically mixed audiences in Venetian theatres meant that opera served no absolutely distinct high- or low-class group. For much of the seventeenth century, when Venetians imposed their own style on Italian opera as a whole, the artistic results were very marked. Various features of opera at Venice—the excellent stage productions and the good singing, for instance—reflected the taste of aristocratic and princely patrons. Other features reflected popular influences—particularly comedy and farce, which were not originally in opera supported at court but which rulers soon found to their liking.

Much attention has been given in the past to the disposition of the auditorium in Venetian theatres,[4] and rightly so, since the introduction of the box system there affected architectural plans for many other European opera houses and produced further artistic trends in opera itself. There is some evidence that the concept of private boxes as part of a theatre plan was dawning in Bologna some years before the start of Venetian opera. A description of the old Teatro della Sala of 1615 in Bologna states that on the north and south sides of the interior ran 'three rows of balconies supported and divided regularly by pillars rising from a base three steps above ground level'.[5] Whether the balcony sections marked by the pillars were separated inside to create boxes is not clear. A description in 1639 of the rebuilt Teatro della Sala refers definitely to 160 *ponti* (i.e. boxes),[6] and we can see how easily the balcony arrangement changed into the other.

Old pictures of the inside of a theatre during an opera sometimes show the ruler, or chief guest, seated upon a dais at the front of the auditorium.[7] This was clearly a good vantage point. The increasing popularity of boxes, however, meant in many cases the move of the highest class from the floor of the auditorium upstairs. This increased both the social and financial value of boxes enormously. In Venice and other towns where the same system operated, boxes could be rented for the night or—as was commonly the case—for the season. The custom of attending for the season can be explained only by the fact that boxes were used more often to entertain privately than to observe the show. A box in other words was like a small reception room at home, and rich habitués of the opera finally began to regard it as a family privilege to be passed, like a house, from one generation to the next. The Venetian Republic seems to have encouraged the box system. State policy laid down that members of the foreign diplomatic corps were not to fraternise freely with the local nobility, and ways and means had to be discovered of seeing that they were well entertained in recompense. The best gesture was to give foreign embassies a box in each opera house. Jean-Jacques Rousseau, who was secretary in 1744 to the French ambassador to Venice, described in his *Confessions* how the system worked while he was there. At this time the ambassador had a box in each of five theatres and 'at dinner he announced which of them he intended to visit that evening. I [Rousseau] had the next choice, and the gentlemen disposed of the other boxes'.[8]

Before passing on to the bad effects of renting boxes, we could well defend the custom, first of all on the grounds that it ensured the perpetuity of opera as such in a great number of theatres in Venice and elsewhere which would not have performed it other-wise or would have given it up after a short while. A society that had got accustomed to entertaining in the theatre continued to prefer a background of opera to any other. However, more than social prestige and the ability to entertain was at stake in the survival of the box system and thus in many cases of opera itself. When demand for boxes was high, their financial value rose. If a theatre was burnt down—a common hazard—then the invisible assets of the box-holder vanished with it. In such circumstances the tenants were often the ones to put the most pressure on the owners or on the political regime to have it re-erected. An instance was the destruction of the theatre inside the ducal palace at Milan in 1776 followed by requests from box-holders and other interested persons to the government for an immediate replacement.[9] Such was the interest and demand that two new permanent theatres were en-visaged, of which the larger is now the world-famous La Scala. Box-holders provided a large proportion of the funds needed for the new building and seem to have paid gladly since erection costs were less than the market price of their box privileges.

Certain aspects of the system were perfectly innocuous and even amusing. Tenants could furnish boxes in the way they chose, just as they would a room in their own houses. Stendhal noted this custom in Rome in the early nineteenth century, though it un-doubtedly went back many years:

It is the custom here for every patron to decorate his box according to his own peculiar fancy; one may observe curtains looped and tasselled as for a window in Paris, and balconies tricked out in silks, velvets or muslins; some of these inventions are absurd to a degree, but there is pleasure to be had in the very variety. In three or four instances, I perceived draperies so disposed as to suggest to the distant beholder the form of a *crown*; and upon enquiring, I received the explanation that this strange artifice affords a sort of consolation to the vanity of certain still-crowned but desperately impoverished heads, whose owners continue to eke out their declining years in Rome.[10]

The trouble was that the privacy a box afforded encouraged tenants to turn their attention away from the stage towards social intercourse, cards and other idle pursuits. Samuel Sharp, an English visitor to Naples in the 1760's, recorded what went on in the fashionable S. Carlo theatre:

The *Neapolitan* quality rarely dine or sup with one another, and many of them hardly visit, but at the Opera; on this account they seldom absent themselves, though the Opera be played three nights successively, and it be the same Opera, without any change, during ten or twelve weeks. It is customary for Gentlemen to run about from box to box, betwixt the acts, and even in the midst of the performance; but the Ladies, after they are seated, never quit their box the whole evening. It is the fashion to make appointments for such and such nights.[11]

Such inattentiveness was a concomitant of much of the noise and chatter that usually accompanied performances. Italian opera patrons became particularly turbulent over the years and in the eighteenth century achieved notoriety through the hubbub they raised.[12] Those now accustomed to go to an opera and listen without distractions of any kind should realise that the general public's habit of listening avidly to an entire performance has been comparatively recently formed. It may be claimed that Wagner both through his music and through his productions at Bayreuth, a town too far out of the way for other than opera enthusiasts to attend, did more than anyone to get the public listening properly. Seventeenth- and eighteenth-century audiences, on the other hand, did not visit commercially run theatres with that sense of devotion to a composer that characterised Wagner's followers. In these earlier centuries audiences knew that it was they who controlled opera; it did not control them. The noise and hullabaloo that they created every so often, when there was no autocratic enforcement of

discipline, was an unthinking demonstration of the fact. The great
misfortune was the bad effect of such inattentiveness on opera
itself. The less the audience cared, the less artists were prompted to
create works of consistent dramatic coherence. In Italy especially,
artists swam with the tide by developing forms of opera which had
moments of intense brilliance but which did not command continuous attention from the audience. The recitative suffered most,
since this was the part least listened to.

The part that Venetian theatres played in the history of opera
was therefore a complex one. In the seventeenth century their
commercial organisation and the artistic quality of their product
were highly influential factors in the growth of operatic projects
elsewhere—at Hamburg, for example, where the first commercial
opera house in Germany was opened on the Goose Market in 1678.[13]
This ran regular seasons of opera, most of which was in German, for
a period of fifty years. The Imperial Free Cities, of which Hamburg
was one, had internal self-government, and some eighteenth-
century visitors thought the living standards of the ordinary
citizen higher there than in neighbouring autocratic states. Burney
on his tour of 1772, however, was in no doubt which of the two
political systems produced the best music:

> Whoever therefore seeks music in Germany, should do it at the several
> courts, not in the free imperial cities, which are generally inhabited by
> poor industrious people, whose genius is chilled and repressed by penury.[14]

Cities relying heavily upon trade were, apart from Venice, less
likely to spend fortunes on entertainment than the courts. Hamburg's opera house was an exception. It competed for fame with the
few court theatres, such as those of Weissenfels and Wolfenbüttel,
that staged opera in German, and seems to have influenced commercial ventures in other cities. Certain aspects of the Hamburg
opera—the wide range of society attending the theatre, the consequently broad range of appeal of the work performed, and the
close artistic parallels of its productions to the Venetian—tend to
make comparisons between Hamburg and Venice inevitable. The
Hamburg public, however, lacked wealth on quite the Venetian
scale and was not swelled by the particularly large international
gathering that thronged south for the Carnival. Unfortunately,
too, it was not absolutely united in its approval of opera, partly
on religious grounds. Of other factors that perhaps played their

part in the termination of the regular run in 1738, the growing
Italian influence was important, exemplified by the theatre manage-
ment's difficulty after *c.* 1700 in deciding whether to promote its
own distinctive type of opera or a local variant of Italian. It had the
same problem to face as administrators of other German theatres.
The large number of Italian librettos translated and used again in
Germany, of Italian operas performed there without alteration, and
of Italian composers working there, were all signs that fashions were
temporarily weighed against the establishment of a characteristic
German art-form.

The influence of the general public on the shape and style of
opera was much more active in the early eighteenth century than
it had previously been. This was a period when various comic
opera companies sprang up, most of them small, that made
astounding headway in spite of official apathy or resistance. Such
companies acted primarily before bourgeois audiences, though
exceptions may be thought of: *The Beggar's Opera* in London in
1728, for instance, received the enthusiastic support of many
members of the nobility. In the case of Germany, the support of
the middle class for these companies meant a new basis for the
growth of opera in the vernacular. In Italy, where opera in the
vernacular was the norm anyway, their preferences meant a
definite split between comic and heroic, or popular and aristocratic, forms. A contemporary change in the literary climate of
Italy, and the emergence of new classically inspired, heroic librettos
identified with the aspirations and taste of the upper classes, brought
about a middle-class reaction in favour of bourgeois comedy. An
end had now come to the peculiar form of Venetian opera moulded
to please mixed audiences consisting of all grades of society. In
France, too, heroic and comic operas were now separate, the second
emerging especially at the *Comédie italienne* and on the Parisian
fairgrounds to dispute the hold the *Académie royale* had over the
opera of the nation.

Comic opera was at first performed mainly in the inexpensive,
non-privileged theatres or taken round by travelling groups to
halls and private houses.* Consequently, it seldom had the fine

---

*cf. K. von Dittersdorf, *The autobiography*, English ed., London, 1896, pp. 37–8,
for a description of a troupe's visit to Schlosshof, the Austrian country seat of Prince
Joseph Friedrich von Hildburghausen, in the early 1750's:

. . . . a certain Piloti, manager of a troop of actors, drove up to the village inn,
with his wife and another actor, and asked to see the Prince. On being introduced, he

trappings of aristocratic or court productions. Burney, who came to Naples in 1770, complained that the singing and drama of two comic operas he saw there were bad.[15] He had to admit, however, that other features, the good acting and especially the tunefulness of the music, made up for the deficiencies. His report gives a good clue to what audiences expected to receive from comic opera. The features he mentions, plus the comedy, were the vital ones which stimulated the public's interest. If spectators did not listen, then of course they missed the joke and the fun which others were enjoying. The inference is that they were involved in the stage drama to a degree which audiences in some high-class, privileged theatres were not. The inattentiveness of society at the Neapolitan S. Carlo theatre* was certainly detrimental to the development of good drama. The public's greater involvement elsewhere in comic opera probably affected it for the better.

By the late eighteenth century comic opera, in Italy at least, had gained the edge in artistic quality over its heroic rival. Equivalent forms abroad, such as *opéra comique* and comic *Singspiel*, had acquired equal maturity. The not surprising result was a quickening of interest in such works among the upper classes and a switch from their previous allegiances. Comic operas—in Italian if they preferred to keep the traditional language of court operas, or in the vernacular of their own countries—were now inserted into the schedule of courts and high society. The new phase may be related to the policies of the eighteenth-century age of Enlightenment, when rulers made a show of appreciating and even following popular artistic tastes. It may also be thought of as the conclusion of a cycle of operatic history. Opera, after having been transformed and altered to meet popular demand, had once again returned to being a court art.

Comic opera.

said that he was acting in Pressburg from November until the end of May, but that, in the summer, he and a few of his company were on tour through the smaller towns of Austria . . . After mentioning a number of comedies, he added that they were ready with the 'Serva padrona' of Pergolesi; it had been performed over thirty times in Pressburg, by general desire . . . With his wife, and one actor, he could perform the Intermezzo that very day, and they had brought proper dresses expressly for the purpose. Although the other two were Germans, and the manager himself was only half an Italian, they all spoke with the best accent . . . They selected for the temporary theatre a coach-house, built on so grand a scale by Prince Eugene that it had all the look of a *salon*.

*See p. 40.

1 S. Towneley Worsthorne, *Venetian opera in the seventeenth century*, Oxford, 1954, p. 28.

2 A list of seventeenth-century Venetian opera houses is in A. Loewenberg, *Annals of Opera, 1597–1940*, Geneva, 1955, cols. 15–16.

3 *The letters of Mozart and his family*, ed. Anderson, London, 1938, i, 155.

4 cf. Towneley Worsthorne, op. cit., p. 24.

5 C. Ricci, *I teatri di Bologna*, Bologna, 1888, pp. 29–30.

6 ibid., plate facing p. 32.

7 cf. *Denkmäler der Tonkunst in Österreich*, vol. III(2), 1896, plate facing p. viii.

8 J-J. Rousseau, *The confessions*, bk vii (years 1743–4), Penguin edn, London, 1963, p. 289.

9 C. A. Vianello, *Teatri, spettacoli, musiche a Milano nei secoli scorsi*, Milan, 1941, pp. 111 ff.

10 Stendhal, *Rome, Naples and Florence*, English edn, Calder, London, 1959, p. 457.

11 S. Sharp, *Letters from Italy, describing the customs and manners of that country*, London, 1766, p. 82.

12 ibid., p. 81. Also *Dr Burney's musical tours in Europe*, ed. Scholes, London, 1959, i, 66–7.

13 cf. H. C. Wolff, *Die Barockoper in Hamburg*, Wolfenbüttel, 1957, 2 vols.

14 *Dr Burney's musical tours*, ii, 42.

15 ibid., i, 241 and 248–9.

4

ARTISTIC ORIGINS

The origins of opera can be traced not merely to one source but to several. Classical studies and influences, and a host of different artistic currents, were moving in its general direction during the sixteenth century. The interests of the group particularly connected with the first operatic experiments, the Florentine *Camerata*, were both scholarly and progressive. Its researches into the past were tied up with speculations on practical problems that included the future of the arts. One idea shared by many of its members was that the ancient Greeks had sung or musically intoned the texts in performances of their tragedies. Although this idea was never proved to everyone's satisfaction at the time, its influence over those *Camerata* artists interested in shaping the course of music and drama was profound. Even if the *Camerata* itself had not existed, other academies with strong scholarly and artistic interests abounded which might eventually have thought of drama set to music throughout. Various sixteenth-century arts were developing on lines which, viewed in retrospect, seem to have moved conclusively in the direction of opera.

Those wishing to examine other possible sources of origin may turn back to medieval liturgical and mystery dramas if they wish. One of the earliest operas, Cavalieri's *Rappresentazione di anima e di corpo*, performed in Rome in 1600, may be considered a remote descendant of these because of its obvious didactic intent and religious overtones. Other more immediate predecessors of opera included sixteenth-century revivals and imitations of ancient dramas, pastorals, and Italian court comedies with inserted entr'actes called *intermedii*. These *intermedii* had little dramatic substance but were popular because of their music and because of those magical, glorious and spectacular scenes previously described in connection with *Il rapimento di Cefalo*, one of the earliest operas.* In fact *Il rapimento* may be thought of as an emancipated and developed group of such entr'actes.

The growth of the concept that different arts should be closely interlinked and related was an important element in the situation, since, if opera was to come into existence at all, poets had to believe that their dramas would benefit from musical setting throughout, and composers that their worthiest aim should be to enhance the expression and meaning of words. Both groups had ultimately to make some sacrifice to the independence of their position. This was not lightly done, and required a high degree of sophisticated thought on both sides.

Classical studies suggested that music had been used in ancient times as an expressive aid to the recital of poetry. Some sixteenth-century poets were intrigued by the idea of a new, close liaison between the two arts, and had the opportunity in academies and other gatherings to meet musicians and discuss with them how music and poetry could more closely serve a common purpose. Of these academies the *Académie de musique et de poésie* founded in Paris in 1570 is worthy of special mention. This society became known for its experimental *vers mesurés*, poetry in which vowels possessed strong accentual and quantitative differences and therefore a strong rhythmic stress. The aim was almost to give the poetry a musical, if highly variable, 'beat' so that the musical stress in any musical setting was predetermined.[1] *Vers mesurés* were set to music by Claude Lejeune, Jacques Mauduit, and other composers of the society, and have been described as the first step towards French recitative.[2] The irregular rhythms of this music are a characteristic of songs, or *récits*, of later French ballets, and finally of recitative proper found in the operas of Lully and his successors.

This *Académie* is also credited with having influenced the design of the first great *ballet de cour: Circé, ballet comique de la reine*, 1581. The creators of *Circé* retained the customary and very miscellaneous elements of ballet but fitted them all, in a way that had never been done before, into a dramatic and well-arranged scenario. The aim of the director, Beaujoyeulx, was not to produce

*See pp. 22-3

a work with music throughout. His idea of merging several arts into a joint scheme nevertheless had something in common with that of later opera writers. His preface shows his attitude:

... j 'ay animé et fait parler le Balet, et chanter et resonner la Comedie: et y adjoustant plusieurs rares et riches representations et ornements, je puis dire avoir contenté en un corps bien proportionné, l'œil, l'oreille et l'entendement.[3]

Since the French court had a penchant for dancing and mime, it was hardly likely to be the first sponsor of opera with fairly continuous singing. Opera had more chances of appearing first in Italy where singing was, and still is, considered a natural and everyday form of expression. Before the first operas Italian poets and musicians experienced, like their French contemporaries, a growing sympathy for, and understanding of, each other's art. This was fairly general and by no means confined to the *Camerata* in Florence. Their growing understanding had its effect on their work and created a climate in which opera could come about.

The 'musical' qualities of late sixteenth-century Italian poetry involve more than the sounds and rhythms of the language. Even more important is the emotion that the poetry describes and evokes; an emotion that is at one and the same time highly pathetic and exaggerated. The pathos of this poetry is not genuine passion. All the same, the very exaggerated way in which it is expressed elevates it artificially to the rarified realms of pure feeling; on such rarified levels poetry most nearly approaches the spirit of music. Such highly elevated and therefore, in a sense, 'musical' feelings can be traced in this verse set by Luzzasco Luzzaschi as a five-part madrigal which appeared in 1594:[4]

> Dolorosi martir, fieri tormenti,
> Duri ceppi, empi lacci, aspre catene,
> Ov'io le notte e i giorni hor'e momenti
> Misero piango il mio perduto bene.
> Triste voci, quereli, urli e lamenti,
> Lagrime spesse e sempiterne pene
> Son'il mio cibo, e la quiete cara
> De la mia vita, oltr'ogni ascenz'amara.

It is no mere chance that the earliest librettists usually turned for inspiration to those forms of drama in which poetry of this kind

occurred regularly. The pastoral drama, exemplified by Guarini's
Pastor fido and a popular genre in the late sixteenth century, contained both delectable poetry in a pastoral idiom and poetry full
of pathos. It was the most suitable type of drama for through-
composed musical setting. The dramatic scenes set to music by
Cavalieri and mentioned in the preface to *Rappresentazione di anima
e di corpo*[5] as having been acted before the Grand Duke of Tuscany
in the 1590's were short pastorals. Their successors, the operas
Dafne and *Euridice*, performed in 1597 and 1600 respectively with
words by Rinuccini, had scenarios based on ancient myths but
dressed in pastoral guise. This means that both they and the pastoral
drama proper were set in an idyllic world of innocence and pleasure,
and that both had a bare modicum of action generated by the
passion of love. Love, unrequited or incapable of satisfaction, gave
the impulse to those many expressions of torment, self-pity and
sensuality, which aroused musicians to write their most passionate
music and which listeners admired. Furthermore, poets emphasised
the agonies of love so that their work could gain a high degree of
seriousness commensurate with the standards of classical drama. The
pastoral drama was clearly intended to possess some of the emotional
and charged qualities of tragedy without in every case having to
embrace those of its features, such as the tragic ending, that the
sixteenth century sometimes found unacceptable. Certain characteristics obviously imitated Greek tragedy; the use of messengers as
narrators was one. The entry of a messenger to tell a tale of disaster
involving the chief characters allowed for less action on stage than
would have been necessary had the event been seen, and for more
emotional verse during the telling. The earliest operas retain this
convention. Messengers arrive to narrate the tragic occurrences, for
instance Silvia's entry to give the news of the death of Euridice in
Monteverdi's *Orfeo*, 1607, and their words are key moments of
eloquence.

The requirement that vocal music should interpret the text was
accepted by all Italian composers of the second half of the sixteenth
century, though there was some confusion whether 'interpretation'
meant detailed word-painting or a more general, emotional musical
counterpart of the text. In the long run the expression of emotions
was felt to be a worthier and more subtle aim. This was part and
parcel of speculation at that time about the various 'humours' and
passions. This subject keenly interested students of the arts, philo-

sophy and medicine. In the world of music theorists set out to analyse the passions and state how composers could simulate them in their compositions. Hence the gradual rise of the 'doctrine of affections' which by the time it had reached its peak of elaboration in the early eighteenth century was a large catalogue of emotions and of compositional techniques to convey them to the listener. The doctrine was to be a useful guide to composers when they set words since it suggested techniques that would, in theory at least, mirror the emotion of the text correctly. A work like Orazio Vecchi's *Le veglie di Siena*, a madrigal drama of 1604 with the significant subtitle *i varii umori de la musica moderna*, shows signs of the gradual formulation of the doctrine at the beginning of the seventeenth century. The drama's second section consists of fourteen madrigals of a Profound (Grave) nature simulating in turn the following 'humours': Serious (Grave), Cheerful (Allegro), Universal (Universale), Mixed (Misto), Libertine (Licentioso), Sorrowful (Dolente), Agreeable (Lusinghiero), Kind (Gentile), Affectionate (Affettuoso), Treacherous (Perfidioso), Sincere (Sincero), Alert (Svegghiato), Melancholy (Malenconico), Eccentric (Balzano). Monteverdi in the preface of his eighth madrigal book, 1638, talks of three main 'affections': the Soft (Molle), Moderate (Temperato) and Agitated (Concitato), and usefully states his method of producing a *stile concitato*, or agitated style, calculated to affect the listener.[6]

The growing conviction in some quarters that vocal music should heighten the meaning of words went hand in hand with another: that the words had to be clearly heard or the setting had little value. Count Bardi, a most influential member of the *Camerata* and its host for several years, came out strongly *c.* 1580 against vocal polyphony in which the words were likely to be swamped. In his *Discorso sopra la musica moderna* he told the composer and singer Giulio Caccini: 'In composing, then, you will make it your chief aim to arrange the verse well and to declaim the words as intelligibly as you can.' He then added significantly: 'not letting yourself be led astray by the counterpoint'.[7] His bugbear was really the severer polyphonic styles, of the earlier part of the century especially, in which the several voices declaimed separately and the text was lost in a complex of pure sound.

Yet, during the period when Bardi was writing, secular vocal music in several parts was fast ridding itself of elaborate polyphonic devices which bore absolutely no relation to the words at hand

and were simply a sign of the composer's ebullience and prowess. In the theatre there was a growing tendency towards vocal ensembles rich in sonorities but without contrapuntal intricacies of any kind. An extreme case of simplification of style was the severely homophonic choruses of Andrea Gabrieli in the version of *Oedipus Rex* by Sophocles produced at Vicenza in 1585.[8] Here lyricism was so reduced that the style, dependent largely on rhythm and harmony, was close to psalmody. Homophonic styles, of which this was an extreme example, eased the problem of ensemble vocalists concerned with getting their words across to an audience. Only in simple monody was there still less problem of clear diction.

The sixteenth century had always been conscious of the beauty of monody, as historical records of 'solo' vocal performances testify. The style of early *frottole* suggests that they were intended to be performed as vocal solos with instrumental accompaniment,[9] while the numerous transcriptions of vocal polyphonic pieces into solo songs add proof of this form of music making. The declamatory style of certain late sixteenth-century Italian madrigals made them also suitable for transcription. Luzzaschi's *Madrigali . . . per cantare, et sonare a uno e doi e tre soprani*, which appeared in 1601 but were probably composed some years previously,[10] were actually published with a keyboard accompaniment replacing the customary lower parts. Three of these madrigals were for a solo soprano. This signifies a trend towards solo song in the madrigal at a time when, during the 1580's and 90's, the *Camerata* were making their first experiments with monodic recitative accompanied by *basso continuo*. The *Camerata*'s pieces were therefore not entirely isolated from the monodic trend in Italian part-music. The madrigal and operatic monody continued to influence each other after the birth of opera, and shared stylistic points in common. Monteverdi arranged his famous monodic Lament from *Arianna*, 1608, as a five-part madrigal; yet the latter in no way suffers from being an arrangement and could easily be taken for a composition originally conceived for five voices.

Parallel too with the first experiments in the direction of opera ran the movement towards the madrigal drama, in which groups of madrigals were joined together either to provide the outline of a comedy—and it was only the outline since there were obvious gaps in the story—or to suggest a social occasion such as a banquet or festival with successive entries of entertainers to sing, crack jokes, and act miniature plays. Madrigal dramas were popular with those people who felt that the trend towards greater expressiveness in vocal music had gone far enough in the many several-voiced madrigals of the period, and who wished to hear semi-dramatic works in which nevertheless the traditional, polyphonic standards of composition had been preserved. It was not the normal custom to act such dramas. The number of vocal parts in the madrigals did not fit the number of characters anyway. A work like Vecchi's famous *L'Amfiparnaso*, published in 1597, is clearly for the ear and relies upon the powers of poetry and music to suggest the theatrical setting.

The preface to Adriano Banchieri's *Saviezza giovanile*, 1607, states that a method adopted in another of his madrigal dramas had been to put singers and instrumentalists behind a curtain and two actors in front.[11] If this was a technique to preserve a perpetual flow of polyphony as an accompaniment to visual action of some kind, it had very limited uses. A play sung in monody was the obvious final choice for those composers wanting continuous music to support drama in a way that seemed relatively natural. Madrigals could occur, if need be, in the play's choral sections. The point was that the type of monodic recitative evolved by the *Camerata* allowed the singers individually to open their mouths and act as they would in contemporary spoken drama. Several-voiced madrigals usually surpassed monody in purely musical value but were no substitute for it in through-composed music dramas with individual characters. The *Camerata* wished to ally music to words and gesture in the most natural manner. Instructions in Cavalieri's score of *Rappresentazione* tell the singer to interpret his part by emphasising the emotions, using both forte and piano but no superfluous ornament;

and in particular he must pronounce the words clearly so that they be understood, and accompany them with gestures and movements not only of the hand but also of the feet, so that his actions contribute to the affection.[12]

Here we have the biggest advantage of early opera over mere semi-dramatic forms such as the madrigal drama. The new musical experiments in opera could be *seen* to have some relevance, however attractive or unattractive they might be in themselves; and, since opera contained elevated verse and the whole range of technical stage devices that madrigal dramas did not, there was no doubt which of the two would outdistance the other.

1   cf. F. Lesure and D. P. Walker, introduction to *Claude Le Jeune*, *Airs (1608)*, American Institute of Musicology, 1951, vol I, pp. viii ff.

2   H. Prunières, *Le ballet de cour en France*, Paris, 1914, pp. 62–3.

3   ibid., p. 84.

4   Words and music in A. Einstein, *The Italian madrigal*, Princeton, 1949, iii, 257–61.

5   A. Solerti, *Le origini del melodramma*, Turin, 1903, p. 3.

6   O. Strunk, *Source readings in music history*, London, 1952, pp. 413–15.

7   ibid., p. 295.

8   Reprint, ed. L. Schrade, Paris, 1960.

9   Einstein, op. cit., i, 76–7.

10 ibid., ii, 845.

11 F. Vatielli, *Arte e vita musicale a Bologna*, Bologna, 1927, p. 68.

12 Solerti, op. cit., p. 5.

SEVENTEENTH-CENTURY ITALIAN OPERA

Music had a function in opera distinct from any it had had in previous drama. Instead of occurring merely at selected emotional or picturesque moments, music in opera was continuous and had to support both the most elevated and the most mundane sections of the text. The association of music with the more mundane sections of drama was a novel one for the period.

Peri's music to *Dafne* is unfortunately lost, though we can tell from the score of his next opera *Euridice* what the earliest operatic music was like. Striking features are the baroque figured bass, which here makes one of its first appearances, and more especially the predominant recitative-like monody. Although this monody has more musical attributes than the stereotyped *secco* recitative of later years, its slow and irregularly moving bass and its speech-song style combine to give it few of the qualities necessary to make it enjoyable simply as music. The point is that much operatic monody was hardly considered music even by its composers. It was a type of speech-song such as, so the *Camerata* conjectured, the Greeks might have used in the distant past. Peri, in the introduction to *Euridice*, provides the clue when he wrote that in his opinion the ancient Greeks

had used a harmony surpassing that of ordinary speech but falling so far below the melody of song as to take an intermediate form.[1]

The implication was that some of his music was also an 'intermediate form'. Occasionally indeed his style seems more rhetorical than musical.

This is not to deny that his recitative is sometimes expressive. Peri was aware of the need to vary the emotional depth of recitative and to imitate sympathetically changes of intensity in the text. An excellent instance is the moment in scene ii when Dafne enters to announce the death of Euridice. With the increase of pathos goes a slowing down of the pace.

Ex 1   *Peri*, Euridice, *scene ii*
                                        (*Publ. Marescotti, Florence, 1600*)

ORFEO

E per te Tir-si mio ri-me-ni il so-le   sem-pre le not-tee i

DAFNE ritorna in scena sola

dì lie-ti e___ ri-denti.___   Las-sa   che di spa-ven-to   e di pie-

-ta - te   ge-la-mi il cor nel se-no   mi-se-ra-bil bel-ta-te

com' in un pun-to   ohi - me   ve-ni-sti me - no.

Occasionally the style changes completely and a short song or chorus occurs. Such differences are to be noted not because they destroy the musical unity of the work but because they betray the composer's occasional and quite natural inclination to expand the scope of music beyond the limits of speech song. The stylistic contrasts are the first trace of two diverging musical streams in opera which become much more pronounced in later years. The speech-song sections, or recitative, are one; and the lyrical sections, or the arias and ensembles, are the other.

Seventeenth-century Italian opera is normally divided into three main types: the Florentine, Roman and Venetian, such labels conveniently describing certain artistic traits common when Florence, Rome or Venice was the chief opera centre. Early Florentine opera of approximately the first decade of the century was in essence perpetual recitative, though it assimilated other, more flamboyant features primarily through court influences. Roman opera in the second to fourth decades had more spectacular and lyrical attributes, being produced with great lavishness and opulence, and written for relatively big casts and choruses. Venetian opera of the fifth decade onwards had a slightly different character, since it was performed in commercial as well as private theatres and therefore acquired more 'popular' qualities than ever: better scenery, more comedy, and more good tunes. But the fact that impresarios of commercial theatres had to work within certain budgets meant at the same time cutting down on some extravagances, notably the large choruses, which had been a feature of operas previously produced in Rome.

Florentine operatic monody has features common also to later recitative. The generally syllabic vocal style, the opportunities for free rubatos and changes of pace, the purely chordal nature of the bass, are among these. Yet early monody has some expressive qualities later recitative lacks. In particular, singers are able to dwell on the end of each cadence—which is written in slower notes, i.e. minims and semibreves, than the rest of the phrase—and wring it dry of pathos. The similarity of such cadences to those in late sixteenth- and early seventeenth-century madrigals is one of several signs that monody borrowed many of its melodic and harmonic formulas from elsewhere. The close stylistic connection between madrigal and monody can best be seen in Monteverdi's monodic *Lamento d'Arianna* and the madrigal version of it in his sixth madrigal book.

Since composers gave no directives when monody was to be sung in free and when in strict time, we have to guess the degree of strictness of the tempo from the style. In early opera the accompaniment, which is usually just a figured bass, often gives the clearest indication. A bass with motivic work, or with regularly moving minims or crotchets, suggests a strict pulse; a slow or irregularly moving bass a free pulse with possibilities for rubato. The change in the bass part from irregular to regular movement really implies a change from recitative proper to what is generally termed *arioso*—this is music in a free, lyrical style—or to aria. Another indication as to whether monody is to be performed in strict tempo is the time signature. From the very beginning the more declamatory sections were customarily composed in $\frac{4}{4}$ time. A signature of three semibreves or minims, therefore, nearly always implies a lyrical style with a regular pulse. It goes without saying that singers in an ensemble must maintain a unified and regular tempo.

There is surprisingly little use of triple time in the earliest operas, but then triple time is the exception rather than the rule in the more serious madrigals too. Where it appears, it sounds like a foil to the prevailing common time and tends to have the effect of a change to a more light-hearted and popular idiom. In much the same way the galliard following the pavane, or the saltarello the passamezzo, in dance collections also creates a sense of happiness and gaiety. Triple time is a feature of certain instrumental and choral sections in Peri's *Euridice*, but is generally missing from the monody except where the text expresses a feeling of happiness. Giulio Caccini's version of *Euridice*, published in 1600 but not performed till 1602, contains practically no music in triple time at all. Monteverdi reserved triple time in his *Orfeo* for some of the gayer and more festive moments, following Peri's principle. Act II of *Orfeo* shows the trait clearly. The use of common time throughout long sections of these very early operas can only mean that constant changes of time signature were not then considered necessary, and that other methods of contrast—such as changes of instrumental colour and of emotional level in the recitative—were held sufficient to counteract boredom. The situation was different in the 1620's and following decades when triple time was more commonly used in the lyrical sections.

Recitative proper soon became conventionally set in common

time only. Once the main musical interest passed into the many
ariosos and arias, it became starved of aesthetic qualities of its own.
By the middle of the seventeenth century the lingering cadences of
early recitative had been speeded up, a racy, patterlike style had
come into being, and the previous 'touching' and 'pathetic' moments
—created by sharp dissonances, pauses, short vocalisations and the
like—were fast disappearing. At the same time certain harmonic
progressions and melodic phrases were becoming mere stereotyped
formulas to be used time and time again. By the end of the century
the following types of cadence were constantly employed:

Ex 2

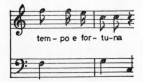

The same formulas must be perfectly familiar to every devotee of
the music of Handel, Mozart and other eighteenth-century composers. The odd thing about these cadences is that the voice finishes
before the accompaniment, and the question is bound to be asked
how such a peculiar, yet common, convention could have come
about. In fact, the device of the vocal part breaking off first had
originally been one reserved for a special effect. Mazzocchi's score
of *La catena d'Adone*, 1626, contains an example of its use indicating
what its original significance probably was. When the witch
Falsirena discovers in III, iii that Venus has wrested Adonis from
her power, she gives vent to her feelings with such vehemence that
they overcome her and she falls fainting to the ground. Here is the
musical passage. Nothing better could have been thought of to
imitate her total collapse than this final cadence:

More interesting than the story of recitative is that of the various lyrical sections and especially the arias. The term *aria* occurred in music before the beginning of opera; for example as a subtitle of the madrigal *Filli, tu sei più bella* in Marenzio's fifth madrigal book in five parts, 1584. For students of opera the important point about this piece is its form. It contains two main sections, each consisting of two closely related musical strophes. The *arie* in Giulio Caccini's important collection of monodies called *Nuove Musiche*, 1602, all contain strophic variations. Strophic form, in fact, seems the point in common between most arias of the late sixteenth and early seventeenth centuries. Arias also occur in the earliest operas, though not all are so-called. Some are lyrical and gay, like 'Vi ricorda o boschi ombrosi'—in Act II of *Orfeo*—which has exact strophic repeats. Others, like the song which forms the Prologue of this opera, are written in a semi-recitative style and contain strophic variations over a fixed bass.

Among the many significant features of Mazzocchi's *La catena d'Adone* is the index of arias printed at the back of the score. It is clear from this that all the major, self-contained items, excluding certain choruses, in the work were considered arias whether they possessed strophes or not, and that even certain choruses were considered arias if they had repeat marks or formed part of a larger strophic item. Once again the word *aria* does not imply a particular style—the phrase 'aria recitativa' was far from being a contradiction in terms such as it would later become. Nor does it necessarily mean a vocal solo since the list includes items such as 'L'alma pure. Aria a 6' and 'Avampando. Aria a 3 soprani' which are for more than one voice. The word may therefore appear all-embracing to the point of mere vagueness. Yet the index implies one basic distinction between aria and recitative—arias have emotive qualities other than those achieved just through musically heightening speech inflexions and rhythms. The large number of arias in this score is in itself a point of interest, and implies some dissatisfaction with recitative and a wish for music with more formal clarity and possibly more lyrical qualities. This dissatisfaction seems confirmed by the remarkable sentence at the bottom of the index: 'There are many other semi-arias scattered through the opera, which counteract the tediousness of the recitative but which are not mentioned here.' What are the semi-arias? A look at the score shows that they must be the many short lyrical phrases which occur in the midst of the recitative and are like short ariosos.

The inclusion of choruses in Mazzocchi's aria index shows their stylistic connection with other items. In discussing choruses we must first distinguish between monodies for individual members of a chorus—such monodies were not uncommon in the earliest operas which were close to the Greek dramatic model—and the multi-part choruses that formed part of practically every opera until and including those of the early Venetian period. Early seventeenth-century composers of opera whose training and technique allied their styles to those of the previous polyphonic era and whose tastes were not ultra-modern welcomed the opportunity to write multi-part choruses. *Dafne*, an opera performed in Mantua in 1608, shows its composer, Marco da Gagliano, more at ease in the choral than monodic sections. Composers during the Roman period, too, seem sometimes to have set the bulk of their operatic monody without much interest but to have written their choruses with enthusiasm. Some of these choruses, especially those found in the sadder and more poignant moments of Roman operas, have stylistic resemblances to polyphonic madrigals of an earlier age. Some exhibit polychoral techniques. Extra variety was obtained through repeats of a group of short and differently constituted choruses to create an over-all strophic form. The ends of the acts were the customary places for the larger ensembles and therefore became the moments of the maximum musical splendour.

Once the Venetians had drastically reduced the role and size of the chorus, Italian opera by and large did without it. Its only remaining function was the utterance of the occasional battle cry or shout of welcome. The exceptions where it gained greater prominence usually occurred in court operas produced in Vienna or other foreign capitals. The loss of the chorus in Venetian opera was bound to mean, of course, some temporary impoverishment of musical texture. In a way it is surprising that the Venetians should have done this when their own musicians—Andrea and Giovanni Gabrieli, and Monteverdi among them—had built up a fine tradition of choral, and polychoral, performances at St Mark's and other churches. The end to choruses of any size meant that composers were thrown back on other resources to aid musical variety and in particular on their ability to create lyrical arias which solo singers enjoyed singing and audiences hearing.

To understand other factors bearing on the rise of the aria, we must return for a moment to the *Camerata* and its views on vocal virtuosity. Many *Camerata* musicians were expert singers whose vocal skill is reflected in their compositions. Some of their earliest monodies show an extraordinary preoccupation with virtuosity—especially in the *intermedii* to the play *La pellegrina*, 1589.[2] These contain vocalisations and melismas which both make nonsense of the verbal stress and appear too often the music's whole purpose. The style of writing seems quite different from the recitative-like monody of the operas of 1600. Yet Giulio Caccini's *Euridice* is not altogether free of virtuoso embellishment, and we know from the instructions at the beginning of his *Nuove Musiche*[3] that extra improvised decorations and trills were encouraged in renderings of his monodies. The implication must be that the *Camerata* as a whole considered embellishment one of the legitimate ways of heightening expression. The danger was that decoration and expression were terms which could too easily become equated.

Yet vocal virtuosity was not so highly prized for its own sake in the early seventeenth century as, alas, it later became. In the days of early opera florid singing was sometimes considered quite the opposite of mere exhibitionism. Of elaborately decorated songs in early opera perhaps the most famous is 'Possente spirto' in Act III of Monteverdi's *Orfeo*. Here the composer wrote down both a simple and an embellished version of the melody, the second containing various recommended trills and decorations. Such embellishments serve a dramatic purpose. The song occurs when Orpheus' entry into the underworld in search of Euridice is challenged by Charon, the boatman. It is the song of a lifetime— Orpheus using every possible resource of which he has knowledge as a singer to overcome Charon's resistance. The fact that he succeeds is a sign of the superhuman qualities of his song.

Virtuosity in early opera is often a symbol of magic or of supernatural powers. Possibly the ability of singers of the period to astound and charm an audience with embellishments had something to do with this association. Vocalisations and trills are to be found especially in the parts for deities, magicians and allegorical figures. These parts are often short, but are no less technically difficult than those for the chief characters.

This is quite different from the later situation when the more difficult and embellished music was almost invariably allotted to the singers in the chief roles. The turn about began round the middle of the century when deities and magicians were beginning to disappear from Venetian opera. Mid-century musicians were if anything less conscious of the need for virtuosity than their predecessors of the *Camerata*. From *c.* 1670, however, vocalisations and embellishments began to creep into aria styles with a vengeance. The expressive intent behind the virtuosity now became less clear. At the same time the allocation of arias to particular characters was becoming related less to dramatic ends than to the question of giving the singers the solos they wanted. Already in 1669 we find an opera libretto, *Genserico*, which states that various extra arias have been added to please the cast.[4] The number of arias awarded one singer as against another became a symbol of comparative status. It therefore follows that the better singers finally obtained a majority of the arias and with them more occasion for demonstrating their virtuoso techniques.

Mazzocchi's remark about the monotony of recitative gives another clue why arias became popular. The arias had all those

lyrical and rhythmic characteristics that recitative so obviously
lacked. Comparison can be made between arias and other short,
popular pieces of the period, dances among them. The connection
between aria and dance is not surprising considering the popularity
of ballets at court and the artistic closeness of the two genres: opera
and ballet. Some operatic songs accompanied dancing; others were
based on dance tunes heard in the same work. The style of this
aria, from a ballet of the 1620's, was copied in many operas of the
same period:

Ex 4   *F. Caccini*, La Liberazione di Ruggiero, *scene i*
                                    (Publ. Cecconelli, Florence, 1625)

The fashion for triple-time arias, which reached its apex in the middle of the century, was connected with the fashion for certain dances. Sarabande, corrente and minuet rhythms became popular in arias.[5] Later, the $^{12}_8$ time of the giga and siciliana was also used. One of the interesting technical details of these triple-time styles is the *hemiola* or cross rhythm—this can best be described in modern terminology as a temporary change from $^6_4$ to $^3_2$ or from $^6_8$ to $^3_4$—that commonly occurred just before cadences and became a regular device for heralding the close of important phrases (see the setting of the words 'dona amore' in Example 6 below). This technique was still a common one in the early eighteenth century and one constantly used by Handel and others.

The use of triple time, again, led to a temporary situation in which arias in $^4_4$ time were in a minority. These arias also had their 'popular' attributes:

Ex 5   *Cavalli,* Orimonte, *1650, I, viii*
                                        (*MS Venice, Bibl. Marciana 9890*)

FLERIA

Com' io t'a - mi non sò   non sò   non sò   com' io t'a - mi non sò

tro-var di te più fred-do un a-man-te chi può? com' io t'a - mi non sò

non sò   non sò   com' io t'a - mi non sò

This should be compared with the triple-time aria below:

Ex 6   *Cavalli*, Orimonte, *1650*, II, iii
                                (*MS Venice, Bibl. Marciana 9890*)

fuo — re vi___ le — — — ga — -no e tall' hor vi do — — — na a — mo — re___ po-mo guas-to di den-tro e___ bel_____ di__ fuo — re.

Both Examples 5 and 6 are for one of the stock characters of Venetian opera, the *damigella* or female attendant. It does not take long to see that the two arias illustrate two sides of her personality. In the first aria she is simply being her natural, vivacious and un-sentimental self; in the second she is displaying her propensity for satire. Example 6 is a musical parody of the style often adopted by the high-ranking characters of the opera. Its deliberately over-elongated phrasing and slight laboriousness brings into sharp relief certain features absent in Example 5. Some of the musical differences between the two examples can be seen by a glance at the cadences. Italian composers must have observed, both in the seventeenth century and earlier, how cadences gave a brighter effect on certain degrees of the scale than on others. The first of these two arias under discussion has particular vivacity with its single middle cadence on the fifth degree. The second aria by comparison seems to meander; this is in no small part due to the feeling of uncertainty about the next cadence and the degree of the scale on which it should fall. Perhaps wishing to meet demands for lighter, gayer music, mid-

C

century composers gradually began to use certain 'gay' cadence
points more systematically and regularly than they had done in the
immediate past. Their tendency to make their music progress to
specific cadences—on the third and fifth of the scale, for instance—
increased their dawning understanding of key structure. The clearer
this understanding, the more unerringly their phrases moved in the
direction of the right cadence and the more they avoided acciden-
tals which might deflect the music from the right modulation.

The first of the *damigella*'s arias has a vivacity which soon became
associated also with the music of kings, princes, and other high-
ranking characters. By making sovereigns and others pronounce
weighty verdicts in this lighthearted manner, composers increased
the satire and humour of Venetian opera. Other developments in
the aria included the more precise organisation of its musical
material. Arias in Florentine and Roman opera had usually consisted
of two or more verses, each to the same music or with the same
musical outline. Later fashions, however, moved in favour of arias
with one strophe only, its setting developing clearer and ultimately
more rigid structures. One of these new structures was the *ostinato*
bass, which became associated in the minds of some composers
with pathetic laments once Cavalli had written a notable lament
with *ostinato* bass in his *Gl'amori d'Apollo e di Dafne*, 1640.[6] Other
and more common structures were the ABB form illustrated in
Example 6 above and the ABA form illustrated in Example 5.

The late seventeenth-century swing towards the overwhelming
use of *da capo* form in the aria—and towards the virtual exclusion
of all other aria forms in opera in Italy—is a crucial yet puzzling
development. The instruction *da capo* originally seems to have been
used in mid seventeenth-century scores to indicate that an aria had
a second or further strophe. Such phrases as 'Da capo l'aria un'altra
strofa' or 'Da capo l'aria per la seconda strofa' are found relatively
often. Later it became associated with ternary-form arias in which
the first and third sections were exactly the same, musically and
textually. Composers, realising finally that an exact A repeat in an
ABA aria satisfied contemporary taste, came to write the words *da
capo* after the second section to save themselves the trouble of re-
writing the first. It was convenient and frankly a bit too easy. The
very exactness of this repeat in so many arias of the turn of the
century and beyond led to musical monotony and has since then
persistently drawn the critics' fire.

P. F. Tosi, in his *Opinioni de'cantori antichi, e moderni,* 1723, helps the modern age to understand why the *da capo* form was so fashionable in the eighteenth century. A progressively increasing amount of embellishment should, he states, be applied by the singer during the performance of a *da capo* aria. Only simple extraneous ornaments are to be added in the first part; some more artful graces may be introduced in the second; while in the third part—the repeat of the first—considerable variation of the vocal line 'for the better' is required.[7] He who does not embellish this third part, says Tosi, 'is no great master'. The part of the aria that constituted the point of climax was clearly the third, since this was where the singer's creative skill was most actively engaged. From the audience's point of view the simple first part was necessary so that the variants in the third could be properly appreciated. The embellishments were the real *raison d'être* of the whole piece.

There is no evidence to suggest that mid seventeenth-century singers embellished their ternary form arias to any great extent. Other reasons there may be for the initial popularity of the form which, once it had become overwhelmingly popular, then became a vehicle for technical demonstration. The shapeliness of ternary form may in itself have been the most cogent reason why it became so common. Furthermore, an exact *da capo* repeat, like a second strophe, gave audiences the opportunity to hear the same music twice and thus come better to terms with it. The following first section from a *da capo* aria by the Italian composer Agostino Steffani, who spent much of his working life in Germany, might begin to establish itself in the memory of an audience the second time round:

Ex 7 *Steffani,* Henrico Leone, *1689, II, xvii*
(*MS British Museum RM 23 h 6*)

IRCANO

La sfre - na - ta gio - ven - tù la sfre-na - ta gio - ven-

continued/

-tù quan-do il sen-so la fla-gel-la la fla-gel-la la ra-gion non o-de più quan-do il sen-so la fla-gel-la la fla-gel-la la ra-gion non o-de più non o-de più etc.

The term *aria* was not the only one which became associated with opera. *Sinfonia* and *ritornello* were terms applied to its instrumental sections. Opera overtures, and instrumental pieces that had a dramatic function of some kind—music for ceremonial entries, and battles, for instance—normally came to be called *sinfonie*; while the purely musical preludes and interludes to vocal items came to be called *ritornelli*. This difference between the two took time to become absolute, and was in any case usually a functional one rather than musical.[8] Ritornellos at first remained stylistically separate from arias. During the course of the century, however, the originally tenuous connections between the two became firmer; ritornellos became a more normal part of the aria structure and more closely integrated into the aria style.

The number and type of instruments employed in early opera is sometimes a matter of conjecture, and there is even doubt where they were positioned in relation to the stage. The preface to Cavalieri's *Rappresentazione di anima e di corpo* suggests that the instrumentalists should be behind the stage 'so that they should not be seen',[9] though this directive clearly could not apply to those singers who accompanied themselves, in full view, on guitars, lutes and other similar instruments. Singers did this quite often in early opera. To offset the difficulties of ensemble that occurred when the instrumentalists were out of sight, Gagliano suggested in 1608 that they should be positioned where they could see the singer.[10] This seems to imply that they should be in front of the stage.

The scores themselves are generally lacking in indications of the instruments used, though the prefaces occasionally give details. Monteverdi's *Orfeo*, on the other hand, gives more specific instructions, and may be taken as a guide to what happened in other cases. The instruments used here were in three basic groups: first, the wind group of recorders, cornetts, trumpets, trombones; secondly, strings of the violin family; and thirdly, the various *basso continuo* instruments such as harpsichords, regale, lutes and bass viols.[11] This collection of instruments was not an exceptional one for the period, being similar to those used in *intermedii* and musical plays in the late sixteenth century. What is striking is the opportunity for richness and contrast of colour within this ensemble. Even within the *basso continuo* group harpsichords, organs, lutes and double harp, either altogether or subdivided, could and did provide a variety and sumptuousness of sound far removed from the tinkly harpsichord sounds we nowadays sometimes associate with performances of recitative. The changing instrumental combinations are often written into the score, and so give a guide to the instrumentation of other contemporary operas. The remarks in the score of *Rappresentazione di anima e di corpo* that a 'lira doppia', 'clavicembalo' and a 'chitarrone' or 'tiorba', sounded well together; similarly an 'organo suave' with a 'chitarrone'; also that

Signor Emilio (Cavalieri) would be in favour of changing the instruments to accord with the affection expressed by the singer,[12]

tie in perfectly with the evidence of *Orfeo*.

The chief development in operatic instrumentation during the Roman and early Venetian periods was the increasing popularity of the violin family at the expense of the viols and wind instruments in general. The consequence was some general decrease in the variety of instrumental colour. The Italians' particular reliance on the violin family was not strictly copied abroad where the viol family was kept longer in service and wind instruments always maintained their popularity. The scoring of a big court opera like Cesti's *Il pomo d'oro* produced in Vienna in 1667 shows a variety of instrumental colour not found in the average opera produced at Venice. Although early Venetian scores give very little indication of the instruments used, managerial accounts originally belonging to the impresario Marco Faustini and now in the Venetian Archives give us some idea about the instrumentalists engaged in Venetian opera of the 1650's–60's.[13] His orchestral account is very modest and contains specific mention merely of a few string and *basso continuo* players. Additional players may have been called in who are not on his lists, but this is largely conjecture. Stylistic evidence in a few operas suggests that brass and drums were sometimes employed.[14]

When and how were instruments used in operas of the Venetian period? Only in the last decades were there signs that the string orchestra was settling down to playing in the four parts—two violin, one viola, and bass—that later became standard. Previously, five or three parts—the latter corresponding to the trio sonata combination—were usual. Only gradually were instruments other than those supporting the *basso continuo* allowed to accompany the vocal sections of an aria. But once it had become customary for the upper strings and other obbligato instruments to accompany the voice, they had great effect upon the aria's musical character.

It should be explained that for most of the century instrumental styles rarely invaded operatic vocal items. One that occasionally did so was Monteverdi's *stile concitato*, a characteristic of which was a succession of fast repeated notes in the instrumental parts calculated to create a sense of tumult and excitement. The prominent feature of another style was a jogging or prancing *basso continuo* part consisting of a chain of moving crotchets or quavers. The song 'Chi professa virtù' in the prologue of Monteverdi's *L'incoronazione di Poppea*, 1642, is an early instance of its appearance in opera. In the case of the various dance styles found in mid-century opera, their song-like qualities are at once evident. Hence the numerous choruses and songs related to dances. Only in the last decades of the century did obbligato solos for violins, trumpets, or woodwind bring instrumentally conceived idioms regularly into operatic vocal music. Contemporary with this, the virtuoso spirit of the instrumental concerto began to make its impact.

A discussion of the music of seventeenth-century Italian opera is not complete until reference has been made to its influence on the operatic libretto. The measure of music's influence on librettos can be assessed by the number and position of arias, ensembles and choruses in the text; and to some extent by the pace and emotional quality of the language. In the very earliest librettos music served the text as much as vice versa. The pace and layout of Rinuccini's *Euridice*, set by Peri, were conceived of almost in terms of spoken rather than music drama. This text with its balanced structure—divided into three parts, the middle one a scene of Hell, and the first and last a pastoral scene on Earth—is impressive, and needs no music to improve it. The shift towards librettos which contain obvious 'operatic' features begins already in the libretto to Monteverdi's *Orfeo*, 1607, words by Alessandro Striggio, which contains choruses and songs so positioned as specifically to further the musical effect. A cluster of these choruses and songs at the beginning of Act II to celebrate the forthcoming marriage of Orpheus and Euridice, for instance, is arranged in text and music to come dramatically to an end with the arrival of the messenger Silvia to announce the death of the heroine. Her passage beginning

Ahi caso acerbo! ahi fato empio e crudele!,

is sung in poignant recitative which sounds the more pathetic because of its contrast with the proceeding festivities. Silvia's message in *Orfeo* is the same as Dafne's in *Euridice*, yet the two librettists make them deliver it in a different way. Rinuccini makes Dafne take her time telling her sorrowful tale; he treats her exposition as a literary exercise and enjoys the poignancy of the moment too much to rush it. Striggio makes Silvia come to the point more quickly with possibly some loss of fluency in the poetry but with considerable gain in dramatic impact. The new quickness of pace in certain sections of *Orfeo* seems arranged for sharper musical contrasts and suggests that Striggio was writing to suit the composer.

The faster pace may also have been due to the fact that Striggio's scenario was more complicated than Rinuccini's and covered more ground. The part of the legend, for instance, in which Orpheus leads Euridice up from Hades is totally ignored by Rinuccini, whereas Striggio makes the episode the climax of the work. It is a difficult episode to portray convincingly, as those who know the parallel and not entirely satisfying scene in Gluck's *Orfeo* of 1762 will realise. Yet Striggio, and Monteverdi with him, significantly brings this incident on to the stage—it need only have been reported

in the best classical and pastoral drama traditions—and makes of it
a scene famous for its sense of occasion and psychological acuteness.

This tendency to increase the number of incidents seen probably
owed something to the desire of stage designers for more opportunities for spectacle. The occasion, in Rinuccini's version of the
Euridice story, when Venus appears in a chariot drawn by white
doves to offer help to the disconsolate Orpheus is told to the audience
by a narrator. In a similar way the arrival of the god Bacchus on
Naxos is narrated, not seen, in the opera *Arianna*, 1608, for which
Rinuccini wrote the text. Where the theatre had the necessary
stage appliances, however, there was an irresistible temptation to
materialise the supernatural events and so give more opportunities
to the stage designers and technicians. Once it became customary for
such scenes to form a part of the stage production—as happened
almost at once—then the poet's incentive to describe them in the
most moving and beautiful language was gone. There is no doubt
that the poetry of librettos suffered as a result. It is interesting, for
example, that when M. A. Buonarroti described the stagecraft of
Rapimento di Cefalo,* words by Gabriello Chiabrera, his Italian
prose almost took upon itself certain poetic and descriptive qualities
which might have found their way into the libretto of this opera
had the rise of the sun from the waves, and similar events, been
reported, and not seen by all. As it is, the libretto is a dull piece of
writing.

The fashion for spectacle in the early seventeenth century had its
effect upon the scenarios chosen. The legends of Dafne, Orpheus,
Andromeda, Adonis, Proserpina, and others may have been selected
partly because of classical influences;[15] but there is no doubt that
the same subjects also allowed librettists to bring in all the spectacular scenes, the deities and other supernatural characters, that had
previously been popular in sixteenth-century plays and *intermedii*.
In the 1620's further stories with miraculous events suiting the
purpose of stage designers were taken from medieval romances and
epic poems such as Ariosto's *Orlando furioso*, and turned into opera
scenarios. A swing away from the element of the supernatural was
first evident in the 1640's when a new type of libretto, based on
ancient history, became popular. In historical operas the galaxy of
mythological characters was out of place and therefore began to
disappear. Later it was found mainly in court operas with allegorical

*See p. 22–3.

scenes in praise of the reigning monarch. On the other hand, non-supernatural forms of spectacle—parades and battles, for example—always maintained their popularity right through the period this book covers.

Literary trends in Italy in the early seventeenth century also had their effect on the libretto, but in such a curious way as to confirm the tendency for the libretto to become conspicuously 'operatic' and unlike spoken drama. The greater pretentiousness of poetry of that period, its far-fetched metaphors and imagery, and its greater sensuousness, attempted to work further on the sensibilities of readers than the poetry of Tasso and Guarini had done. In the same way, characters in opera of the 1620's expressed themselves in more overwrought imagery than ever. Indeed their passions were so overwhelming as to lead them in moments of crisis to delusions and periods of mental imbalance. Fainting and raving fits became common, while the sight of a character falling asleep out of sheer exhaustion following a bout of hopeless depression was to become all too familiar to seventeenth-century audiences. Librettists' desire to whip up the emotional pitch further meant an end to the slow, easy pace that had been the characteristic of Rinuccini's librettos. Audiences now had to be entertained by a more violent and emotional type of opera altogether. Hence the more strained atmosphere of both language and scenario in opera of the 1620's and 30's. A new lachrymose sentimentality also began to appear. This is evident especially in *S. Alessio*, 1632, with words by Giulio Rospigliosi who later became Pope Clement IX, where certain of the characters are in a perpetual state of dejection and misery from beginning to end.

The increasing emphasis on action and on emotional crises led to decreased reflectiveness and calm appraisal by operatic characters. Composers of the Roman period may well have thought this was to their advantage. Prolonged discussion about which is the better of two alternatives, about right or wrong methods of behaviour, about people's motives, may have its place in spoken drama but will probably be ineffective in opera. With the Italians' early realisation that music drama would not bear a long philosophical or intellectual text, there was an inevitable tendency towards a 'strain and stress' type libretto in which characters acted on impulse and jumped out of one emotional crisis straight into another.[16] At each of these, emotional outbursts were natural and lyrical arias bubbled forth. Musical theory furthered this general trend. Music was, according to the doctrine of affections, a reflection of human feelings and therefore had to have scope to represent them. The increasing number of emotional climaxes in the libretto gave composers the opportunities they sought to highlight different feelings in turn in different arias.

It is against this background that the artistic development of Italian opera becomes clear. The librettist had to ensure a text of sufficiently high emotional pitch to suit musical setting. Ultimately the best type of scenario was felt to be one of intrigue—set against an ancient historical rather than mythical or epic background—in which the major characters suspected their lovers, plotted and spied on each other, eavesdropped, intercepted letters and messages and generally got into a tangled set of personal relationships. Here there was plenty of opportunity for each character to be passionate, revengeful, liable to be hurt emotionally. As in the old pastoral drama, love was the greatest single force behind the characters' actions and caused each one to act wildly without any thought as to the wisdom of the steps taken. The librettist, in fact, simply took him from one bizarre situation to the next; then, at a time when it was convenient for the opera to close, stopped all the intrigues short and arranged a happy conclusion. Dead men were then brought to life, injured men cured, the couples married off as though there had never been dissension among them, and the librettist thereupon considered his work finished.

Spanish drama had its maximum influence over Italian opera during this period. Gio. Francesco Busenello gave a hint of the influence of Spain in the preface of his libretto *Didone*, set by Cavalli in 1641, which states:

This work reflects modern opinion. It is constructed not in accordance with the rules of Antiquity, but according to Spanish methods which permit the years, not just the hours, to be represented.

Plays by Lope de Vega and Calderón were arranged as librettos, and the Venetian fashion for fast-moving intrigue and comedy was affected by the example of the *comedias de enredo* and other forms of Spanish drama. Yet the sheer preposterousness of Venetian librettos marks them in a class of their own. Music was the overriding factor affecting their literary quality.

By the mid-century librettists were sadly coming to the conclusion that they had led themselves, and been led, to develop a type of text that had little to recommend it from the literary standpoint. A new, self-effacing attitude began to find expression in their libretto prefaces. They imply that they have done their best in circumstances they regret and that they could do better if only public taste were different. One librettist, Francesco Sbarra, went so far as to suggest in his text to *Alessandro vincitor di se stesso*, 1651, that opera was an unnatural entertainment because of the various arias that were to be found within it.

I know that the *ariette* [arias] sung by Alexander and Aristotle might be thought unsuitable for such great persons; but I also realise that recitation in music is unsuitable, since it does not imitate natural speech and removes life from the drama which should be none other than an imitation of human actions. However this defect is not only accepted by the present century but received with applause. Poetry (in opera) only serves nowadays to entertain, and one must accept what the times require. If the recitative were not punctuated by similar *scherzi* [i.e. arias], it would cause more boredom than pleasure.

Thus, with a shrug of the shoulders, Sbarra and other librettists set about providing what they concluded the public wanted.

Among the features inserted into librettos partly to suit the taste of the public was the element of comedy. There seems no doubt that comic characters were initially introduced into Roman opera mainly as an antidote to the prevailing atmosphere of strain and stress. Charon, in *La morte d'Orfeo*, words and music by Stefano Landi, 1619, is said to be the first comic character in opera.[17] In *S. Alessio*, 1632, there are three comedians: two pages and a nurse, who are precursors of numerous pages and nurses in Italian opera right through to the early eighteenth century. Rospigliosi, the librettist of *S. Alessio*, seems to have brought them in for several reasons. His story concerns the return of the dying and disguised Alessio, who disappeared the night of his marriage and has since renounced the world in favour of a religious life, to the home of his sorrowing wife and parents. The servants provide witty comments and horseplay to relieve the opera's essentially sorrowful atmosphere. At the same time their extremely down-to-earth remarks serve as a foil to the agitated and impassioned sentiments expressed by Alessio's family. Their realistic approach brings into relief the superior qualities of the family whose steadfast and loving thoughts lead to unrealistic yet 'noble' ventures to find the missing relative. Rospigliosi's object seems to have been to write a libretto demonstrating a case of 'noble' behaviour which would appeal to his by and large aristocratic and clerical audience. The servants in the opera are deliberately shown up for their lack of steadfastness, and indeed of good breeding as their bullying of the beggar, Alessio, testifies.

Influenced by the general atmosphere of gaiety in and outside the theatre, Venetian opera absorbed comedy in rather a different way. The characters are the same servants whom we met in S. Alessio but more and more they appear just for the sake of entertainment. In conformity with the general trend towards comedy, even the chief characters now begin to absorb certain humorous qualities. This situation was relished by those librettists who had pretentions as comic writers. Fully realising how artificial the intrigues in Venetian opera were, they were soon writing parodies of their own work. Prefacing their librettos with remarks about the preposterousness of opera, they put their high-ranking characters—the monarchs, generals, and counsellors—into the most ludicrous situations possible, and everyone laughed with them. The trend began early in the 1640's and spread everywhere where Venetian opera was popular—even into court operas of the period. A work like La finta pazza, words by Giulio Strozzi and music by Francesco Sacrati, 1641, shows it in its early stages. The same opera, revised, was later performed at the French court under the auspices of Mazarin. At the beginning of Act I, Diomede and Ulysses arrive at the island of Sciros to search for Achilles whose help is badly needed in the Trojan war. Thetis, mother of Achilles, has been forewarned of his death by treachery and consequently hidden him away in the court at Sciros disguised as a lady. He has been accepted as one of the ladies in waiting to the king's daughter, Deidamia, and become her secret lover. Diomede asks to see Deidamia, whose beauty he has heard of, and is shown a loggia in which she and her ladies are working. Invited to step forward to receive gifts from the visitors, the ladies troop in and Achilles with them. Accidentally hidden in a garment he receives is a dagger, and it is upon his flourishing this with more than maidenly zest that his identity is discovered. Characteristically, no one stops to assess the situation and ask just what he has been doing—not even Deidamia's father, who packs him off with exhortations to waste no further time and quickly to put on suitable garments of war. So ends Act I, and it is not necessary to go further to demonstrate the strong vein of comedy that is a characteristic of this libretto.

The problem for students of later Venetian librettos is to assess precisely when the librettist was being serious and when light-hearted. There are so many occasions in Venetian opera when an emotional or pathetic incident—including the many 'mad' scenes in which characters have delusions or raving fits—seems too far-fetched to be intended or taken seriously. The humorous intent is quite clear when the kings and heroes shed their dignity and take part in amorous or ludicrous escapades. All notions of ideal kingship are here deflated; the monarchs are reduced to human size and stripped of the aura which, in real life, absolutist propaganda placed about them. Some characters were even modelled closely on living persons; for instance those in *La lanterna di Diogene*, an opera performed at, of all places, the court at Vienna in 1674. A copy of the libretto of this work is now in the Conservatoire at Brussels and contains handwritten notes conveniently stating whom the characters were meant to represent.[18] These included rulers, ambassadors, bishops and papal nuncios, and other high-ranking figures of the period. Venetian opera, in other words, was not an idealised portrayal of court life; rather at times an accurate commentary upon it. So long as no one wanted more than entertainment from opera, it provided those who could see an amusing side to their own lives an opportunity for laughter.

It is when we come to join music and libretto together and assess the over-all result that the basic fault of Venetian opera emerges. This is the big stylistic division, musically, between aria and recitative; and no feature in the libretto could ever hide either the lack of musical cohesion between aria and recitative or the fact that the discrepancy between the emotional appeal of aria and recitative is out of all proportion to the rise and fall in the emotional level of the libretto. The fault gets worse with the passage of time. Musicians seem gradually to have reached the conclusion that the bulk of the dialogue, in which one crazy plot followed another, gave them no chance to shine—hence the fall in the quality of their recitative. Better, they thought, simply to concentrate on what they knew they could compose and sing well: the lyrical arias. The trouble was that recitative, designed to support the bulk of the drama, became merely a bridge between one aria and the next.

Italian opera as a whole became an aria concert—the audience not listening to the majority of the recitative—but with dramatic interludes between each item. This unsatisfactory trend reached its peak in the Neapolitan operas of the eighteenth century which have as a result been roundly condemned by many. Venetian opera, on the other hand, has usually escaped this sort of criticism. It must however bear at least a small portion of blame since many of the failings of later Neapolitan opera have their roots in earlier fashions.

1   O. Strunk, *Source readings in music history*, London, 1952, p. 374.

2   Reprint, ed. D. P. Walker, Paris, 1963.

3   Strunk, op. cit., pp. 377 ff.

4   S. Towneley Worsthorne, *Venetian opera in the seventeenth century*, Oxford, 1954, p. 121.

5   H. C. Wolff, *Die venezianische Oper in der zweiten Hälfte des 17. Jahrhunderts*, Berlin, 1937, pp. 164 ff.

6   A. A. Abert, *Claudio Monteverdi und das musikalische Drama*, Lippstadt, 1954, p. 247.

7   P. F. Tosi, *Observations on the florid song*, English edn, London, 1743, pp. 93-4.

8   E. Wellesz, 'Cavalli und der Stil der venezianischen Oper von 1640-60', *Studien zur Musikwissenschaft* i (1913), 47-8.

9   A. Solerti, *Le origini del melodramma*, Turin, 1903, p. 6.

10 A. Solerti, *Gli albori del melodramma*, Milan, 1904, ii. 69.

11 J. Westrup, 'Monteverdi and the orchestra', *Music and Letters* xxi (1940), 231 ff.

12 A. Solerti, *Le origini del melodramma*, p. 6.

13 Venetian Archives, Scuola di S. Marco, Busta 194.

14 cf. H. Goldschmidt, *Studien zur Geschichte der italienischen Oper im 17. Jahrhundert*, Leipzig, pp. 149-50.

15 A. Solerti, *Gli albori del melodramma*, i. 150-1.

16 cf. Abert, op. cit., pp. 156-8.

17 Charon's song 'Bevi, bevi securo l'onda' is recorded in the *History of Music in Sound*, vol. IV, side 5, band 5.

18 A. Wotquenne, *Catalogue de la bibliothèque du conservatoire royal de musique de Bruxelles, Annexe 1*, Brussels, 1901, pp. 89-90.

6

NATIONAL OPERA: THE FIRST TRIALS

To many a foreigner visiting Italy in the early seventeenth century opera was a complete novelty. John Evelyn, who was in Venice in 1645, found it an art-form sufficiently strange to require a definition in his Diary:

Comedies & other plays represented in Recitative Music by the most excellent Musitians vocal & Instrumental, together with variety of Sceanes painted & contrived with no lesse art of Perspective, and Machines, for flying in the aire, & other wonderful motions. So taken together it is doubtlesse one of the most magnificent & expensfull diversions the Wit of Men can invent.[1]

Through various channels more and more foreigners were coming to hear of this new Italian invention; through the reports of travellers to Italy and of musicians sent there for training, or through the visits of Italians to foreign courts. An early flicker of foreign interest is apparent not merely from the first Italian operas produced abroad but also from early attempts at opera in languages other than Italian—the first opera in German was performed in 1627, the first opera in Spanish in 1629—and from the greatly increased use of music in early seventeenth-century French *ballets de cour* and English masques. However, for one reason or another, drama with through-composed music was too novel an idea to be accepted immediately with enthusiasm, and it really required the next move on the part of the courts: the wholesale importation of opera troupes from Italy, properly to engage the interest in opera of those foreigners who were sympathetic to the use of music in their own theatre. There is thus no doubt that the example of the Italians was the prime incentive behind the start of opera in other languages. The Italians were really giving a practical demonstration of how drama could be set to music throughout, and presenting an unofficial challenge to those few—and it must be stated at once that they were a small minority—who felt that other nations should and could do as well as the Italians in this field. Unfortunately few sovereigns of the period were really sympathetic to their viewpoint. Louis XIV was one of the few who went so far as to give opera in the vernacular secure, official status. His act of authorising an *Académie d'opéra* and later an *Académie royale de musique* was crucial at a time when it hardly seemed likely that non-Italian opera would get going.

The goodwill and active assistance of dramatists and poets was as vital to the start of opera in any country as it had been to the start of opera in Italy. In the experimental first stage, the dramatist's concept was bound to be influential and even decisive. His control over the form and content of opera, and even his power to impede the growth of an operatic tradition altogether, remained strong in those countries where, in the seventeenth century, there was a flourishing tradition of spoken drama. In many cases it was the dramatist who decided whether a play should be set partially or wholly to music, and whether, if the music was not to be continuous, it should be essential to the work or purely incidental.

Many dramatists objected to opera on both practical and theoretical grounds. Those who, like Pierre Corneille, admitted their general antipathy to music,[2] were the least likely to support its growth. Corneille thought that music had a really useful function merely in a small minority of his plays: namely, in those based on classical myth with spectacular scenes where stage machinery was needed. These particular plays were clearly influenced by the stagecraft of Italian opera and even used stage machinery which Italians had constructed. In the preface of his *Andromède*, 1650, Corneille stated his opinion that words sung to music were often badly heard and that it was therefore better to reserve most of the music for moments when dialogue was either unnecessary or inessential.[3] These were mainly the times when the audience was supposedly so engrossed in the stage spectacle that it could not pay attention to the words. Corneille thus wanted music in *Andromède* as accompaniment to the lowering and raising of the machines, and to violent physical action—for instance, the slaying of the monster by Perseus.

The Italian practice of setting all kinds of dialogue in recitative came in for much direct and indirect criticism. Some felt that music as a whole was unsuited to support all types of dialogue and that it should therefore be reserved for when it would destroy neither the naturalness nor verisimilitude of a scene.[4] In Sir William D'Avenant's *The Playhouse to be Let*, 1663, a musician is made to declare:

> Recitative Musick is not compos'd
> Of matter so familiar, as may serve
> For every low occasion of discourse,

and there is reason to believe that this opinion was D'Avenant's own. This writer is important for having written the words of what is generally considered the first opera in English, *The siege of Rhodes*, 1656, the music of which, written by a consortium of composers, is now lost. It has been suggested that this libretto was originally conceived of as a play but then altered and performed with music throughout so that it could be presented in spite of the parliamentary ban on plays then in force.[5] Certainly the scenario of this opera was quite unlike those of Italian operas of the period, having a modern subject based on the siege of the city of Rhodes by the Turks under Solyman the Magnificent in 1522. The work was again performed in the Restoration period, after the ban on plays had been lifted. It may then have been presented as D'Avenant originally intended it, with spoken dialogue replacing musical recitative. There was little demand in London of the 1660's for opera sung throughout.

Perrin was another writer who felt that the Italians were making an error in supposing that texts suited to ordinary recitation could be sung. The Italians, he maintained in a publication of the year 1661, 'n'ont pas trouvé leur conte dans l'expression des intrigues, des raisonnemens & des commandemens graves'.[6] Not knowing of any musical technique which in his opinion could suitably be used in settings of the more mundane and least emotional sections of a drama, Perrin sought his own solution to the problem of writing a text for a through-composed opera. In his *Première comédie françoise en musique*, usually called the *Pastorale d'Issy*, 1659, he thought he had found an answer:

i'ay composé ma Pastorale toute de Pathetique & d'expressions d'amour, de ioye, de tristesse, de ialousie, de desespoir; & i'en ay banny tous les raisonnemens graves & mesme toute l'intrigue, ce qui fait que toutes les scenes sont si propres à chanter, qu'il n'en est point dont on ne puisse faire une Chanson ou un Dialogue.[7]

In fact Perrin's aims here were not so dissimilar to those of the earlier Florentine *Camerata*: to write a work with a very simple libretto allowing for conjunct emotional sequences. Perrin's libretto is significantly a pastoral, and this permitted him to use a diminutive scenario—contained in twenty short pages of text—in which each of three shepherds courts and wins a shepherdess, much to the frustration and rage of an ugly Satyr who also wishes for a wife. This story has even less action and drama than Rinuccini's first libretto *Dafne* and appears even more primitive. The main distinction between *Dafne* and the *Pastorale d'Issy* is that the first was clearly designed to go with the new recitative style of the *Camerata* composers, whereas the second, quite to the contrary, was designed to be set basically in a lyrical, song style. Since the French had not evolved a recitative style of their own that Perrin considered satisfactory as a support for the usual dramatic dialogue of the period, he felt he had to return to first principles and find a type of libretto that would suit the lyrical nature of French music.

The fault of his method was that it could never be more than a temporary answer to the problem of writing librettos. A longer opera would need a more elaborate plot. Thus when he came to write the text for *Pomone*, 1671, the first opera produced by his *Académie d'opéra*, he turned his back to some extent on his earlier principle and chose a much more complicated scenario altogether. Yet his opinions at the time of the *Pastorale* give a valuable clue to the thought of the period. A further clue is provided by the libretto to *Dafne*, translated into German and adapted by Martin Opitz from Rinuccini's text, which Heinrich Schütz set for a performance at Torgau in 1627. The German version removes some of the more turbulent and exciting moments that were a feature of the Italian text and replaces them by new, reflective and lyrical dialogue.[8] The changes seem designed—though the music is lost and final confirmation is therefore lacking—so that the composer's music in turn could be more lyrical and thus less in the purely functional, *parlando* recitative style of the Italians. Hence the translator's deliberate curb on what dramatic variety there was in the original libretto.

The later the attempt at opera in the vernacular, the less chance there was that the results would in any way resemble the first operas of the Italians. The very term 'opera'—a colloquialism for 'music drama' that foreigners took from the Italians around the mid-century[9]—tended naturally to be associated with those most recent Italian works with which foreigners were familiar. After *c.* 1645 late Roman and early Venetian opera became the model which they knew best, and their assessment of opera as an art-form was largely determined by their reactions to opera of this particular type. Features which impressed them included the supernatural elements in the story and the elaborate scenery and machines. All this stage paraphernalia, when introduced into their own productions, of course increased the cost; but then Evelyn had described opera as 'one of the most magnificent and expensfull diversions the Wit of Men can invent' and its very opulence was thought by many to be its chief attraction. Furthermore, the theoretical diehards who believed that music was out of place in most forms of drama felt there were rational grounds for its use in theatre in conjunction with lavish scenery and machines. Music and spectacle together could conjure up a world of mystery and magic, of dreams and unreality, which words by themselves were not so fitted to convey.

In many countries in the second half of the century there was therefore a tendency for librettists to assume that an opera libretto was distinctive from any other sort of dramatic text because it laid predominant emphasis on the supernatural. This particular element is a characteristic of operas produced in Perrin's and Lully's *Académies* in Paris, as it is of the one opera in English which had continuous music and which was produced in the 1680's in a public theatre. John Dryden, the librettist of *Albion and Albanius,* 1685, provided an interesting definition of opera in the preface of the work:

An opera is a poetical tale, or fiction, represented by vocal and instrumental music, adorned with scenes, machines, and dancing. The supposed persons of this musical drama are generally supernatural, as gods, and goddesses, and heroes, which at least are descended from them, and are in due time to be adopted into their number. The subject, therefore, being extended beyond the limits of human nature, admits of that sort of marvelous and surprising conduct, which is rejected in other plays.

This definition to some extent fitted Lully's French operas and also certain late seventeenth-century Italian works produced at court. However, it was quite out of date with reference to the more recent Venetian operas with historical subjects and suggests that Dryden either was unaware of trends in Venetian opera or else chose to ignore them.

Albion and Albanius seems to have been a crucial attempt to create English opera at a time when London audiences were still far from convinced that it was an art-form to patronise. Its first act had originally been envisaged as a prologue to another play and was an allegory on the Restoration of the British monarchy. Acts II and III continued the story of the fortunes of Charles II and of his brother, later James II, but still in the form of an allegory. This made poor drama. The opera's chances of survival were not improved by the music of Louis Grabu, a French composer who had originally come to England around 1665, and whose talent was mediocre. A further blow to the opera's success was the coincidence of its London production with the news of the rise of the Monmouth rebellion in the West of England. London audiences promptly lost all interest in *Albion* and it was withdrawn.

While political circumstances and the taste of the public may not have been conducive to the rise of opera in England, the attitude of the dramatists was partly to blame. Their belief that the music could become more important than the words gave them little enthusiasm to write verse specifically for musical setting. Thomas Shadwell's preface to his *Psyche*, 1675, a drama containing music by Matthew Locke, affects an air of extreme casualness, as though the author really wished to disown this particular play altogether.

I doubt not but the Candid Reader will forgive the faults, when he considers, that the great Design was to entertain the Town with variety of Musick, curious Dancing, splendid Scenes and Machines: and I do not, nor ever did intend to value myself upon the writing of this Play.

Dryden, in the preface to *Albion and Albanius*, confessed he had to overcome his prejudice at writing verse which would count for less than the music it was set to. He declared he even had difficulty in finding words with the right 'propriety of sound' for opera. The problem of selecting a musically-sounding vocabulary seems to have troubled him again when he came to revise his drama *King Arthur* for a production, *c.* 1691, in which sections were to be set to music by Henry Purcell. 'In many places', he complains in the dedicatory epistle, 'I have been oblig'd to cramp my Verses, and make them rugged to the Reader, that they may be harmonious to the Hearer.' Although he praises Purcell's music and declares he is happy to let his art be 'subservient' to the composer's on this occasion, his complaint of 'cramping his Verses' does nothing to dispel the impression that he regarded writing poetry to be set to music as a tiresome business.

The most interesting thing about both *Psyche* and *King Arthur* is that they fit that curious category of late seventeenth-century musical plays in England which Roger North called 'semi-operas'.[10] The printed edition of Locke's music to *Psyche* names the work 'The English Opera', and the composer defends this title—although the music is not continuous—on the grounds that the work has characteristics in common with Italian operas which

after much consideration, industry and pains for splendid Scenes and Machines to Illustrate the Grand Design, with Art are composed in such kinds of Musick as the Subject requires.

According to Locke there was no continuous music in *Psyche* because England was not a centre for this practice. He has therefore 'mixt it with interlocutions, as more proper to our Genius'. None of these remarks disguises the fact that *Psyche* is more a play with music than an opera. Only a relatively small proportion of the total text is sung—a smaller proportion even than in certain English masques of pre-Restoration times—and the sections which are set are for specific characters with short though sometimes significant roles. The principal characters speak throughout. Music is an essential element of all those sections of the story that have an atmosphere of unreality and enchantment or demand luxurious stage spectacle. They include: the entries of the gods, the furies and the devils; the scene in the Underworld; the celebrations in honour of the gods and incantations by their priests. Our conclusion must be that the combination of music and sumptuous décor was considered the essence of 'opera', not continuous music.

This conclusion seems confirmed by other semi-operas, set by Purcell: *Dioclesian*, 1690; *King Arthur*, 1691, *Fairy Queen*, 1692; *Indian Queen*, 1695; and *Tempest*, 1695?; all of which contain spoken dialogue for the chief characters. The purely divertissement character of many of the musical episodes cannot be disguised, though the music fits expertly in with those larger than life moments in the story where magic and enchantment intervene. There is always the feeling that music will break in at any time, since the element of surprise—the sudden and capricious interference of gods and magicians in the affairs of ordinary mortals—is a key characteristic. The scenarios of these semi-operas therefore develop against a background of improbability and music together. The criticism must be that the musical episodes remain too often isolated and uncoordinated not in relation to the plot but to each other. *Dioclesian* is to some extent an exception where the musical episodes occur at first sparingly, then closer together; become longer and more elaborate structures; and culminate in a final masque which is the longest and most elaborate section of all. This masque is technically an epilogue but is without doubt the musical climax of the work. *Dioclesian*, in fact, starts as a play but ends as an opera, i.e. with music the controlling force.

Such semi-operas served as the English version of opera. Besides *Albion and Albanius* the only English operas of the late seventeenth century which had through-composed music were Blow's *Venus and Adonis*, *c.* 1682, and Purcell's *Dido and Eneas*, *c.* 1689, both relatively short works, both lacking in the requirement of stupendous stage spectacle, and both intended not for the public stage but for private performances by primarily amateur singers. As such they were outside the main cultural stream. In other countries, too, there was a tendency to reject opera sung throughout in favour of plays with music; nowhere more so than in Spain where through-composed opera seems to have been promoted but failed to elicit court or public enthusiasm, and where instead the *zarzuela*—a type of heroic drama with spoken dialogue and with episodes in which music and spectacle went together—became fashionable round the mid-century.

The 1660's were a period when it seemed unlikely that opera would gain any foothold in France either. The French court had soundly rejected Italian opera and seemed unshakable in its traditional liking of ballet. The composer later to become famous for his operas in French, Lully, was partly engaged during this period on music for Molière's plays. Dramas in which the two collaborated have sometimes been grouped together under the heading of *comédie-ballet*, though this title was used by Molière himself only in the case of *Le bourgeois gentilhomme*, 1670. Lully's usual contribution was the setting to music of certain short divertissements or entr'actes in which he himself often acted. Their later joint works show some advance in the use of music for dramatic ends. The musical episodes achieve comparative length. In *Les amants magnifiques*, 1670, the third musical interlude or *intermède* is almost a minute opera on its own, being a pastoral with a short prologue and five scenes. Yet this is still a far cry, dramatically, from the later, large *tragédies lyriques* of Lully's *Académie*. Although Lully's cooperation with Molière may, from a historical standpoint, be interpreted as a move in the direction of opera—especially since examples of his operatic recitative style may be found in the last of their plays[11]— there is no evidence that in the 1660's Lully was thinking of establishing French opera. What probably turned his thoughts in that direction was the foundation in 1669 of Perrin's *Académie*.* Perrin's move was really a public proclamation that the problems of founding a French style of opera were not insoluble and that he was going to be the pioneer in this sphere. His action may have piqued Lully into wondering if he could find his own solution; and once the patent had changed hands, the realm of opera was Lully's to occupy.

The problems Lully faced when he wrote his first operas were similar to those experienced by other composers starting opera in any language. Few problems, relatively speaking, were attached to the writing of songs and choruses for which there was ample precedent in the theatre. The moments difficult to set were those where it was not dramatically appropriate that characters should burst into full song. The Italians' answer had been recitative at times 'below the melody of song', but this classically inspired solution does not always seem to have met with enthusiasm in all countries in the seventeenth century. Foreigners' antipathy to recitative may have been partly the result of their hearing chiefly Venetian opera in which recitative had lost much of its expressive quality.

The earlier the attempt to create opera in the vernacular, the greater the likelihood that foreigners would catch the true spirit and style of early Florentine recitative. The opera *Seelewig*—a type of morality play set to music by Sigmund Staden in 1644, and the oldest surviving opera in German—contains some recitative passages reminiscent of Florentine models. Yet *Seelewig* is interesting because

*See p. 28.

it shows its composer's reluctance to write a work largely in an
Italian-style recitative. The considerable use of simple, strophic
forms, plus the rather square-cut two- or four-bar phrasing, gives
much of Staden's music a hymn-like quality with similarities to
certain contemporary German *Lieder*. The tendency to a song style
has obvious connections with trends in other non-Italian operas of
the century.

Precisely what song style should be adopted varied according to
the opinions of the composer, though most mid-century musicians
seem to have agreed with librettists that they should keep the quality
of their music above the level of mere speech song. In the last
decades of the century, however, the Germans gradually began to
compose their recitatives in the latest Italian style, at the same time
adapting this style to the heavy accents of their language. The
English moved more cautiously. When, in the early eighteenth
century, Roger North argued that operas of his day suffered from
too great a stylistic division between recitative and song, and that
he would therefore choose

to quit the *recitativo*, or at least the manner of it, and conduct the whole
opera thro' a continued current of ayre, as in the elder Itallian operas . . .
and *recitativos* . . . were used,[12]

he was in fact enunciating a principle that English composers of the
seventeenth century seem to have obeyed. 'Ayre' clearly meant for
North not just song, with concise forms and phrasing, but free
arioso also. In a work like Blow's *Venus and Adonis* the combination
of song and *arioso* creates a constant high level of musical lyricism
such as the Italians themselves rarely if ever attempted in their
operas. Anyone who waxes enthusiastic over *Venus and Adonis* for
this reason, however, should reflect that it is very short and therefore compares rather with Italian cantatas than with full-length
dramatic works. Purcell's *Dido and Eneas*, the other short English
opera of the late seventeenth century, shows some signs of a change
towards the Italian operatic principle of placing the main musical
interest in the formalised songs and arias. Yet Purcell's recitative is
still far from the conventional, patter type written by Italians of
that period and later.

The death of Purcell, 1695, and the beginning of Italian opera in
London in the first decade of the eighteenth century put paid to all
chances of the growth of an English opera tradition. The early

eighteenth century was a period of Italian operatic domination almost everywhere. The French were the ones who, having been blessed with the foundation of a national opera company and of a national style of opera, obstinately refused to give these up in favour of imported opera from the south. What the French composed and produced must be the next matter for discussion.

1   *The Diary of John Evelyn* (June, 1645), ed. de Beer, Oxford, 1955, ii, 449–50.

2   J. Tiersot, *La musique dans la comédie de Molière*, Paris, 1921, pp. 17–18.

3   E. J. Dent, *Foundations of English opera*, Cambridge, 1928, pp. 48–9. Also Tiersot, op. cit., p. 23.

4   cf. St Evremond, *Oeuvres meslées*, London, 1705, ii, 103–4.

5   Dent, op. cit., p. 65.

6   P. Perrin, *Les œuvres de poésie*, Paris, 1661, p. 281.

7   Perrin, op. cit., p. 282.

8   H. J. Moser, *Heinrich Schütz, his life and work*, English edn, St Louis, 1959, pp. 393–6.

9   E. J. Dent, 'The nomenclature of opera', *Music and Letters* (1944) xxv, pp. 132 ff. and 213 ff.

10   *Roger North on music*, ed. Wilson, London, 1959, p. 306.

11   H. Prunières, *Lully*, Paris, 1910, pp. 94–5.

12   *Roger North on music*, p. 274.

TRAGÉDIE LYRIQUE AND OPÉRA BALLET

The royal patent permitting Lully to found an *Académie royale de musique*, 1672, placed him in an unassailable position to manage the fortunes of opera in the largest and most powerful country in Western Europe. By bringing opera under central control Louis and his advisers were not concerned with their personal supervision of it. The king, unlike certain other autocrats of the period, was no enthusiastic supporter of opera in general, and his personal interest seems to have been confined to Lully's operas alone and did not extend to those of other composers. His policy regarding opera was a manifestation of absolutist principles that the arts should be part of the state organisation. In practice the granting of the patent gave immense powers to the holder, Lully, but also brought heavy responsibilities and a great challenge. The failure of Perrin's *Académie d'opéra* must have convinced Lully that the holding of a patent was no sinecure. He had to found a company and produce works that would satisfy both the court and the general public—no small task in a country where opera was yet to be properly established.

Lully and his successors holding the patent were not limited to any particular type of opera they might produce, nor to its scope or size. The term 'opera' was generally understood to include all stage works with through-composed music. Lully's work for the *Académie* can be classified under the headings of heroic opera (*tragédie lyrique*) and ballet, ballet being a more loosely assembled work than an opera and with little dramatic cohesion between its various episodes or *entrées*. Some of Lully's ballets were performed

at court in the traditional manner with members of the royal
family and the nobility among the dancers. On the *Académie* stage
the same works were acted by an all-professional cast. The slightly
bigger *opéra-ballet*, introduced after Lully's death at the turn of the
century, was close to ballet in form, though it had lost the intimate
court connections and was not intended for amateur performers.
Attempts were made in the eighteenth century to give a more
coherent plot to each of the individual *entrées* or acts of *opéra-ballet*,
though the lack of strong ties between one *entrée* and another still
remained and different parts of the work could be switched round
or replaced by new ones in later productions. Lully's successors
also patronised comic operas[1] and in 1752 even went so far as to
invite an Italian troupe to perform its own brand of lighthearted
opera in their theatre—with the most startling political and artistic
repercussions (see pp. 142–4).

The *Académie* was always mindful of popular taste. Lully's
operas have often been represented as the embodiment of court
fashions, and it is absolutely true that they appealed to the French
court with their elegance, their personification of virtue and
heroism, and their glorification of Louis himself in the prologues.
However, the same works were also intended for the Parisian
public, and a number of them became great popular successes.

Popular appeal had also been Perrin's aim in his first opera for the
Académie d'opéra founded in 1669. *Pomone*, 1671, set to music by
Cambert, was called a *Pastorale*. Although its characters do conform
to certain basic types familiar in other pastorals, the work is in
reality a fast-moving comedy. Vertumne, the *Dieu des Lares, ou
Folets*, has magical powers to change the scene, his own shape and
other people's, at any moment he chooses; and he employs this bag
of tricks to bamboozle and defeat his rivals for the love of the
goddess Pomone. The opera is a magnificent exhibition of magical
transformations, of practical jokes and buffoonery. None of the
visual metamorphoses would have been possible without the stagecraft that the Italians had earlier demonstrated at the French court.
In other respects, too, there seems some connection between
Pomone and Italian opera—for instance, the appearance in *Pomone*
of an old nurse who clearly has Venetian forebears.

When Lully and Quinault set about their first *tragédie lyrique*,
they too seem to have thought in terms of a work with spectacle,
fast action, supernatural surprises, and a touch of comedy. *Cadmus*

et Hermione, 1673, is far removed from the type of heroic opera they later evolved. In this work Cadmus rescues Hermione from the power of a giant by following the orders of heaven to kill a dragon, sow its teeth, and from the soldiers who spring up where the teeth were sown collect an army to do battle with the giant. However, constant interventions by the gods turn the drama into one in which human beings appear merely the playthings of an arbitrary providence. The battle that should ensue between Cadmus and the giant never takes place because Pallas Athene suddenly turns the giant and his followers into stone. Saved by Cadmus, Hermione is then snatched away by an irate Juno, and Jupiter has to intervene to restore her. There is a great deal of external action in all this, but not much development of a human, emotional drama.

The comedy in this opera is provided by two servants: Hermione's nurse, and Arbas, the follower of Cadmus. The nurse has the usual 'Venetian' qualities of shrewdness and directness of speech, while Arbas displays a Papageno-like wit and inclination to run at the slightest hint of danger. The inclusion of comedians such as these was quickly felt to be an anachronism in a so-called *tragédie lyrique,* and after *Alceste,* 1674, they are not to be found in Lully's operas.[2] The banning of comic features is but one of many indications that heroic opera was beginning to be closely influenced by French classical tragedy. There was clearly a desire in influential circles to see a more elevated type of opera that might stand comparison with contemporary spoken tragedies; and it seems to have been Quinault's response to criticism to write librettos with more obvious dramatic and classical qualities.

The problems of amalgamating the accepted main features of opera and French classical drama were considerable; and the success of Lully and his librettist colleagues, of whom Quinault was chief, in finding an artistic solution must be rated one of their most outstanding achievements. The things commonly expected from opera and other forms of musical theatre—stage machinery, scene transformations, battles and triumphal marches, ballet divertissements, for instance—were simply not to be found in the tragedies of Corneille and Racine, Corneille's *tragédies à machines* excepted. Neither of these two great tragedians was usually concerned with visual spectacle and visual action. Their plays demonstrated moral issues: the inability of a man to escape fate or vengeance, or the conflict between a man's better and his worse judgment. Action was limited, as in many a Greek tragedy. When Quinault determined to write librettos more on classical lines, he had in practice to slow down the pace of action, simplify the plot, and present his chief characters with acute dilemmas which they, through temperament or external forces, would find difficult to resolve.

Atys, 1676, shows the classical influence very clearly. It dramatises the story of Atys, who secretly loves Sangaride, the daughter of a river god, but is himself loved by the powerful goddess, Cybele. As the plot develops, he gradually realises that he is on the horns of a painful dilemma, since his own personal inclinations are totally opposed to those of the goddess, yet he dare not openly rebuff her. His consequent anger and frustration, and his acts of folly, lead him inexorably to his doom. Cybele, finally realising that he does not love her, sends him mad; he kills Sangaride and is then turned by Cybele into a tree.

The librettist synthesises 'classical' and 'operatic' features by combining a single tale of trial and adversity with stage effects and *divertissements*. A myth was chosen as scenario again so that there should be plenty of those visual surprises and spectacle customary at the time. Included in the display scenes were the many choral and dancing interludes which had been traditional in French ballet. These scenes presented their own problems to the librettist. In previous ballet they had usually been pure entertainment, a simple delight to eye and ear, and there was little precedent for setting them into the middle of French tragedy. *Atys* and other later works of Lully, however, show how well such *divertissements* could be fitted into a scheme of heroic opera.

Scenes of jollity with dancing and choral singing could in fact increase dramatic tension if placed in opera at the right moments. One critic has correctly written: 'French opera is not a form in which the progress of the action is the sole source of interest. It consists in a succession of tensions and relaxations obtained by pathetic scenes alternating with festivity.'[3] The festive scenes in practice have their most dramatic significance when followed by others in which fortunes appear reversed and the festivities premature. Sometimes a tragic event, the moment, say, in Act II of Monteverdi's *Orfeo** when the death of Euridice is announced, is made to seem particularly pathetic because of its suddenness and

*See p. 71.

because the previous festivities had created an illusion of perpetual happiness, of resistance to change. An excellent example of how a divertissement could be employed to good effect occurs in Lully's *Phaeton*, 1683. The chief character of this opera, Phaethon, is spurred on by the desire for glory to ask his father, the god Apollo, for permission to drive his chariot in the sky. Various portents have foretold disaster for Phaethon, but he is blind to all warnings. Act IV ends with a series of dances and festivities in his honour as he arrives at his father's palace; and his good fortune continues in the first part of Act V when he appears in the sky in his father's chariot and triumphantly proclaims his superiority over his mortal enemies. However, this period of celebration and happiness is simply a prelude to tragedy, for the chariot then goes off course and he is pitched out and killed by Jupiter's thunderbolt. To seventeenth-century audiences, who would have known their classical legends and therefore the ultimate fate of Phaethon well, the festivities before his downfall must have appeared as a fine piece of dramatic irony, a quality which effectively occurs in opera for the first time in Lully's work.

French poetry gave composers peculiar problems. With accentual and quantitative differences in French so much dependent on syntax and expression, the rhythm of French poetry often seems incapable of coinciding with a regular musical pulse; hence much French vocal music of the seventeenth and eighteenth centuries has a fluctuating beat with variable time signatures from section to section or from bar to bar. Lully's particular merit was to regularise the till then anarchical methods of setting French poetry, with its irregular rhythmic bias, by observing and producing a style that approximated to the declamation of actors in French tragedy. It is said that he paid particular attention to the speech delivery of the actress La Champmeslé who had been coached by Racine.[4] He was therefore attempting, perhaps unconsciously, to create that which the *Camerata* had also aimed at: a musical style modelled on the recitation of actors. Lully's recitative in fact sounds like an imitation of stylised declamation rather than natural, spoken dialogue. It is not sung *rubato*, though an illusion of free time is provided by the changing bar-lengths; and its very sensitive pitch-variations to accord with different vowel sounds, plus its *arioso* style, also distinguish it from most contemporary Italian recitative.

French musical influences on Lully's vocal music affect more than the recitative, being especially evident in the short, rhythmically incisive songs, many of which are related to contemporary dances. While many Italian arias of that period are also inspired by dance idioms, the identification of song with dance is more immediate in French opera, where the two so often occur side by side and the one is a faithful, musical replica of the other. The free combinations of solo recitative, *arioso*, and song in parts of Lully's operas, on the other hand, are reminiscent of Italian practices—though of an earlier period in the century—as are the triple-time styles adopted in many of the lyrical sections. It should be remembered that Lully was himself of Italian origin and that he was perfectly familiar with Italian compositions brought into France in the late 1640's and in the 1650's.

Because Italian singers had made themselves so unpopular in France during Mazarin's period,[5] Lully determined to perform his operas with an all-French cast. This was a natural decision to make, though it happened to have far-reaching consequences which he could not have foreseen. Having rejected Italian singing from the beginning, the *Académie* continued to reject it thereafter. In the eighteenth century the technical failings of French singers, and their poor showing by comparison with the Italians, was to be one of the chief stumbling blocks to foreigners' enjoyment of opera at the *Académie*. In Lully's time, however, there were strong political and moreover musical reasons for having local singers. Lully's natural inclination was not towards an ornamental or florid, but towards a simple, monumental style especially effective in tragedy. French singers were perfectly adequate to the demands he made upon them, and there was no need whatever to call in singers from outside.

French audiences for their part liked simple tunes. While Italians of the period usually went to their opera to hear good singing, the French got into the habit of going to theirs not only to hear but also to sing themselves. This gives an important clue to the different values placed on opera by the audiences of the two nations. Dryden is one who refers to singing in the auditorium at the French Opera:

> In France the oldest man is always young,
> Sees operas daily, learns the tunes so long,
> Till foot, hand, head, keep time with every song:
> Each sings his part echoing from pit and box,
> With his hoarse voice, half harmony, half pox.[6]

Addison testifies to the same practice in the early eighteenth century:

> The chorus, in which that opera abounds, gives the parterre frequent opportunities of joining in concert with the stage. This inclination of the audience to sing along with the actors, so prevails with them, that I have sometimes known the performer on the stage do no more in a celebrated song, than the clerk of a parish church, who serves only to raise the psalm, and is afterwards drowned in the music of the congregation.[7]

Precisely when French audiences began this habit can only be surmised, though it was certainly encouraged by those many tunes of Lully which were popular and easy to sing. The great popularity of his music is shown by the remark of the German composer, Georg Philipp Telemann, that foreigners 'could sing by heart whole scenes of *Atys*, *Bellérophon*, etc.', but that they could not remember Italian arias nearly so well.[8]

Lully's success was due not merely to his popular tunes but also to his competent characterisation and to his ability to relate his music to the dramatic situation. In the early operas, *Cadmus* especially, the secondary characters tend to have the livelier airs and the more lyrical and tuneful music generally. As was the case in early Italian operas, the main characters, on whom the main burden of the drama falls, are made to express themselves primarily in emotional recitative and *arioso*. But the chief characters in some later works demonstrate their personalities in the more popular song styles as well, none more so than Phaethon, whose recklessness and youth are expertly portrayed in a series of vivacious airs, many in fast, triple time:

Ex 8   *Lully*, Phaeton, *IV, ii*
                                              (*Publ. Ballard, Paris, 1683*)

The slow pace and limited action of the more mature Lully operas gives the chief characters much time to unburden themselves of their private sorrows and their feelings of love. As Lully grew more assured in his setting of French verse, and his own style became more lyrical, his characters were made to expand their feelings in a series of emotional *ariosos* and songs which are among the most beautiful items he wrote:

Ex 9   *Lully*, Phaeton, *III, i*
                                 (Publ. Ballard, Paris, 1683)

continued/

D

Pha - e - ton, est - il pos - si - ble que vous so-yez sen-si-ble pour une

au - tre que moy? Ah!_____ Pha - e - ton, est - il pos-

- si - ble que vous m'a - - yez man-qué de foy?

While the chorus plays a major part in obtaining those effective dramatic contrasts which were so essential to the over-all scheme, nevertheless it rarely exhibits its own dramatic character. The fact that the chorus appears in many guises throughout the operas is a hindrance to its establishing itself as a strong personality, and when it does so—for instance, in the temple scene of *Cadmus*, III, vi, where the repeated choral cry 'O Mars, O Mars, Mars redoubtable' builds up a sense of urgency and strong feeling—the moment is soon over. The point is also that the creators of *tragédie lyrique* could not help looking upon the entry of a chorus from the choreographic standpoint. Lully had himself been an excellent dancer. Since dancing was considered an essential part of opera and an important aid to expression, the crowd usually entered to dance as much as to sing. The dances are, with the exception of the big chaconnes, short and musically pleasant pieces, but there is no doubt that their qualities are decorative and their contribution to the build-up of the character of the chorus generally negative.

Lully's instrumental sections, too, seem to have a decorative rather than descriptive or pictorial function. There are none of those marvellous orchestral descriptions of sea storms, earthquakes, battles, etc., that become a feature of later French operas and of Rameau's in particular. Lully's instrumental interludes often sound uninspired, though his overtures are interesting musically and are also historically important for their slow-fast, two-section formula which became standard in the French overture until approximately the middle of the eighteenth century. It is because Lully employs his full body of strings, rather than merely the *basso continuo*, to accompany particular songs that some clue is given to the sort of associations the sounds of an orchestra were thought to evoke. These items include in the main songs of sorrow and of sleep, or songs with some association with magic or the supernatural. Other composers influenced by seventeenth-century French opera, e.g. Purcell, tended to use their full string orchestra for similar purposes.

Lully used freely alternating instrumental groupings of *basso continuo* alone, of trio combinations (two high parts and *basso continuo*), and the full orchestra in five parts. His five-part style has come in for much criticism on account of the rather rigid way the parts are handled. Since, however, Lully's band was a large one and there were several players to a part, a fairly tight, homophonic style was essential at that time to ensure perfect precision.

Lully's orchestra was in fact famous for its united attack and general discipline, and there is no doubt that its standards affected orchestral playing elsewhere. Lully, with his large orchestra, was one of the first to experiment with contrasts of tone between the full orchestra and solo trios of strings or wind. He also alternated small vocal groups with the full chorus. Tutti-solo contrasts are often associated with Corelli's *concerti grossi*, though Lully's experiments came first. Once again we note that this particular technique of Lully is a decorative rather than a formal device; yet it shows one of the many links between him and the future.

Lully was so successful in founding a national and popular style of opera that the *Académie* was not free of his influence for a long time to come. Operas by younger composers were inevitably compared, and usually detrimentally, with those of the master. The general position of the younger generation of composers was weakened at the turn of the century and during the first years of the eighteenth by attacks led by clerics and intellectuals on the alleged immorality and unnaturalness of opera.[9] The argument of Le Cerf in his *Comparaison de la musique italienne et de la musique française*, pt 2,

1705, did no good to their cause either. He suggested that the onus of judgment of new works be put on the 'peuples d'honnêtes gens' and others who should compare the new with music known to be good, i.e. Lully's.[10] The generally defensive attitude of the French towards their opera was not cured by the gradual realisation that, while Lully's work had influenced music in England, Germany, and even Italy in the late seventeenth century, Europe's taste in general from the beginning of the eighteenth swung decisively in favour of Italian music and Italian opera. Clearly something was wrong, and Frenchmen engaged each other in acrimonious argument over the merits and demerits of their opera and its favourable or unfavourable comparison with the Italian type.

The early eighteenth century was a period when Italian musical influences began to find their way into French opera once again. This is evident particularly in the songs closely modelled on Italian arias which the French termed *ariettes*; in some more light-hearted operas even arias in Italian are found. Significant of the general trend is the sentence at the bottom of the index of airs in the 1724 printed edition of André Campra's *opéra-ballet*, *L'Europe galante*, first performed in 1697:

> Dans la longue expace de Temps que cette Piece a été representée, on y a adjoûté plusiers Airs Italiens qui se trouvent dans le Recueil des meilleurs Airs Italiens; ainsi il ne les faut point chercher dans la Table cy-dessus.

However, the French might have absorbed such influences to more positive advantage—while yet preserving the individual quality of their own opera—had they been less concerned with keeping the Lully tradition alive. Much less mindful of the past, eighteenth-century Italians were simply not interested in other than new operas and seldom thought of producing a work that was even fifteen years old. Lully's operas of the 1670's and 80's, on the other hand, were still produced on the stage of the *Académie* in the 1730's and even beyond. The battles in the 1730's and 40's in Paris between the supporters of Lully's operas and those of the new master of French music, Jean Philippe Rameau—the struggle between the so-called Lullistes and Ramistes—can only be brought into perspective when it is realised that the then *Académie* seasons included works by both composers. The audience could thus directly compare the two and take sides accordingly.

Much of Lully's method appealed to Rameau who more than

once made plain his admiration for the older composer. He wrote in the preface of his *Indes galantes*, 1735:

> Toûjours occupé de la belle déclamation, & du beau tour de Chant qui régnent dans le Récitatif du Grand Lully, je tâche de l'imiter, non en Copiste servile, mais en prenant, comme lui, la belle & simple nature pour Modèle,

claiming here that his modernity was justified because he was following the true spirit of Lully's operas rather than their style. His phrase 'non en Copiste servile' leaves no doubt about his belief in his own capabilities, and very great in fact they were. But while he was a composer endowed with more natural gifts than Lully, being a naturally good contrapuntalist, a progressive orchestrator, and possessing a flair for pictorial and descriptive writing, he was not a man whose gifts were best suited to the composition of heroic opera. Rameau and his librettists were happy to use many of the basic Lully techniques to good advantage, but such techniques were used because they were the standard practice and well understood rather than because he and his colleagues were particularly intelligent in their use of them. By Rameau's time much of the edge of the classical spirit in French literature had been blunted, and his librettists do not seem to have been able to present him with the sort of cogent, well coordinated heroic text with which Quinault had presented Lully. While part of the blame may rest with Rameau's librettists, he himself must take a share of it for his willingness to accept what was offered and for his habit of revising his operas— sometimes to the detriment of the dramatic sense. In fact, his most satisfactory music for the theatre is in his *opéras ballets* and short ballet acts where an intelligently formulated dramatic scheme is not so essential and where his often highly attractive and voluptuous music may be enjoyed for its own sake.

One difference immediately noticeable between Lully's work and Rameau's first *tragédie lyrique* which appeared in 1733, *Hippolyte et Aricie*, is the change in orchestral style. Certain features of the Vivaldi-type concerto style—fierce tuttis, rushing scales, semi-quaver and demisemiquaver repeated note patterns—are all imitated by Rameau and other French composers of his period in certain obviously pictorial passages descriptive of volcanic eruptions, thunder, the appearance of monsters and other manifestations of irate nature or of the supernatural. Rameau was adept at creating other pictorial effects such as the sounds of the sea, bird calls, or the gentle murmurings of the Elysian Fields; and his tendency to pictorial writing even occasionally extended itself to the overture, for instance to that of the *acte de ballet*, *Pygmalion*, 1748, where the strings imitate the chipping sounds of the sculptor at work on his statue. But Rameau does more in the overture to his heroic opera *Zoroastre*, 1749, where it replaces the prologue, till then traditional in heroic opera, and is itself a short tone poem descriptive of the scenario:

La première partie est un tableau fort et pathétique du pouvoir barbare d'Abramane et des gémissements des peuples qu'il opprime; un doux calme succède, l'espoir renaît. La seconde partie est une image vive et riante de la puissance bienfaisante de Zoroastre et du bonheur des peuples qu'il a délivrés de l'oppression.

This overture is in fact in three rather than two sections, and is one of those later overtures of Rameau in which the traditional French form is either abandoned or substantially modified. This particular music, furthermore, is no longer an abstract evocation of the grandeur and seriousness of tragedy—as most French operatic overtures had been—and seems instead to fulfil precisely the function that Gluck later defined in his *Alceste* preface of 1767:

I have felt that the overture ought to appraise the spectators of the nature of the action that is to be represented and to form, so to speak, its argument.[11]

The curious mixture of traditional and modern stylistic elements in Rameau's scores constantly draws our attention to his half-way position in French opera as successor to Lully and precurser of Gluck. The more modern trends in his music—for instance, the considerable use of the orchestra rather than just the *basso continuo* to accompany the various vocal sections including the recitative—are welcome signs that French opera was gradually if slowly developing. Yet his most original and engaging passages were frowned upon in the 1730's and 40's by the traditionalists, and their criticisms give some clue to the sort of change he was effecting. In addition to stating that his orchestra was too loud and therefore drowned the voices, they declared that his music was too prominent generally (thereby upsetting the careful balance between libretto and music achieved by Lully), too learned, and showing too many signs of his

scientific study of harmony.[12] His music may not have endeared
itself at once to certain sections of his audience for yet another
reason: his vocal writing was, generally speaking, less immediately
tuneful and singable than Lully's. Much of Rameau's vocal writing
is florid—possibly Italian influences had something to do with
this—and was clearly intended for professional singers who could
perform elaborate divisions and trills with relative assurance. Such
music was to be listened to, not to be sung, by the ordinary member
of the public.

The great contrasts in certain of Rameau's works between florid
and non-florid vocal writing are one reason for the curious lack of
stylistic synthesis his music shows. Another reason is the anachronism
created by his intermingling traditional and modern idioms. The
point is that, whereas his *ariettes* are up-to-date for their period,
many of his recitatives and short airs exhibit an old-fashioned
technique similar to Lully's. The change from *ariette* to recitative
seems a return to the past. Some may argue that this is merely an
academic point, yet the break in style is something which most
listeners to Rameau's music will quickly recognise. The break is not
so great as that between recitative and aria in Italian opera of the
same period, but the recitative style of Italian opera hardly impinges
upon our consciousness as music at all whereas French recitative
does. French recitative, unlike Italian, sounds like an attempt to
create artistic music and is taken into account as part of the listener's
emotional experience.

The question of traditional and modern styles is inextricably
bound up with that of musical pace. Eighteenth-century styles,
particularly Italian, sound racier, more streamlined, than those of
the previous century. Where Rameau's music appears at all
Italianate—and his idiom resembles Handel's at times—the same
racy qualities shine through. But his slow airs and recitative,
especially those with changing bar-lengths, seem hardly imbued with
this spirit. The contrast between the dances with regular and the
recitative with irregular bar-lengths—a contrast inherent in Lully's
operas—sounds more pronounced in Rameau's than in Lully's case.

When the dramatic scheme allowed, stylistic anachronisms could
still be effective. Rameau's short ballet *Pygmalion* contains a number
of operatic scenes which culminate in a final grand *entrée* with
dances, a pantomime, choruses and an *ariette*. Only the first part
has any scenario: the story of Pygmalion falling in love with his

own creation, a statue, which is obligingly brought to life by
Amour. The scenes which follow are merely an excuse for dancing
and singing. As the drama finishes and divertissement begins, so
the change is subtly reinforced by a change from serious recitative
and air to a lighter, gayer, and rhythmically clearer style. Since there
is no change back again, the music appears to go through a striking
evolutionary process. Thus Pygmalion's last solo is quite different
from his first; he begins with a French-style recitative and ends with
an *ariette* which is remarkably Italianate, with a rhythmically
pulsating bass, long vocalisations, and in a *da capo* form.

The success at the time of *Pygmalion* and similar works did not
convince everyone that French operatic methods were the best
possible. Some in France could not get over the lack of strong
rhythms in traditional French recitative and air. Rousseau, referring
in his *Dictionnaire de Musique*, 1768, to the way musical directors at
the *Académie* conducted by beating the floor with a stick, continues:

. . . sans ce bruit on ne pourroit sentir la Mesure; la Musique par elle-
même ne la marque pas: aussi les Étrangers n'apperçoivent-ils point le
Mouvement de nos Airs.[13]

The exasperation of the Encyclopaedists and others at the con-
servatism of French opera may be sensed from their many pamphlets
published during the so-called *Guerre des Bouffons* of 1752–4 and in
the years following. Charles Burney, who went on his musical fact-
finding tour of Europe in the early 1770's, was another who thought
French opera dull and out of date:

Indeed, the French seem now the only people in Europe, except the
Italians, who, in their dramas, have a music of their own. The serious opera
of Paris is still in the trammels of Lulli and Rameau, through which every
one who goes thither, either yawns or laughs, except when roused, or
amused, by the dances and decorations. As a *Spectacle*, this opera is often
superior to any other in Europe; but, as *Music*, it is below our country
psalmody, being without time, tune, or expression, that any but French
ears can bear: indeed the point is so much given up, by the French themselves, that nothing but a kind of national pride, in a few individuals,
keeps the dispute alive; the rest frankly confess themselves ashamed of their
own music; and those who defend it, must soon give way to the stream of
fashion, which runs with too much rapidity and violence to be long
stemmed.[14]

D*

One year after this statement appeared in print, however, Gluck presented his first heroic opera in French, *Iphigénie en Aulide*, to the Parisian public. And at once those Frenchmen who in opera looked for the type of dramatic cohesion once obtained by Lully and Quinault believed they had found the man who would revive it. Gluck's previous 'reform' operas—with Italian words by Ranieri dr Calzabigi, who had resided in Paris and knew French operatic procedures well—showed his sympathy for the type of dramatic scheme long ago adopted by the French. *Iphigénie* at once demonstrated that the Lullian spirit was far from dead in French heroic opera, whatever Burney might write to the contrary.

1 cf. P-M. Masson, 'Les fêtes vénitiennes de Campra (1710)', *Revue de musicologie* (1932) xvi, 127 and 224–6.

2 The comic *scène infernale* from *Alceste*, IV i, is recorded in the *History of Music in Sound*, vol. V, side 2, band 3.

3 C. Girdlestone, *Jean-Philippe Rameau*, London, 1957, p. 141.

4 L. Racine, *Mémoires sur la vie de Jean Racine*, Lausanne, 1747, pp. 110–12.

5 H. Prunières, *L'opéra italien en France avant Lulli*, Paris, 1913, pp. 141 ff.

6 J. Dryden, *Albion and Albanius*, 1685, prologue.

7 *Spectator*, no. 29 (3 April 1711).

8 Girdlestone, op. cit., p. 206.

9 J. Ecorcheville, *De Lulli à Rameau, 1690–1730*, Paris, 1906, pp. 55 ff.

10 O. Strunk, *Source readings in music history*, London, 1952, pp. 495 ff.

11 Strunk, op. cit., p. 674.

12 P-M. Masson, 'Lullistes et Ramistes', *Année musicale* (1911) i. 203 ff.

13 J-J. Rousseau, *Dictionnaire de musique*, Paris, 1768, p. 51.

14 *Burney's musical tours in Europe*, ed. Scholes, London, 1959, ii, 18–19.

8

OPERA SERIA

In 1690 the newly founded Arcadian Society met in Rome for the first time. Its members, who came together disguised and under assumed names so that artistic problems of the day could be discussed in an atmosphere of the greatest possible equity between all, were officially there to

further scientific studies and reawaken good taste in literature and particularly in vernacular poetry throughout the major part of Italy.[1]

The Arcadian movement, which grew rapidly as branch societies sprang up in Italy and even abroad, affected opera as much as purely literary forms. New or renewed 'classical' trends in Italian librettos may be directly attributed to it, including pastoral and heroic themes, also a stricter observance of the Aristotelian Unities and other signs of the influence of Corneille and Racine. Arcadian influences seem to have given Italian librettists the faith to assert themselves once more as a positive rather than purely negative force on opera. The determination of the best of them, Apostolo Zeno being outstanding, to make the libretto once more a literary form of significance was to have a decisive effect on Italian tragic/ heroic opera (*opera seria*) for the next sixty years or more.

The turn of the seventeenth century brought into fashion a type of libretto with a more coherent and simple scenario than was common in previous decades, and one more didactic in its purpose. Late Venetian opera had gradually whittled down the elements of comedy and the supernatural. It was a fairly simple step forward for

Zeno, whose first libretto appeared in 1695, to cut these out entirely from the majority of his dramas. His object was to raise his librettos to the level of the best tragic plays and elevate the minds of his audience, as was the aim of contemporary tragedians, by demonstrating cases of noble and heroic behaviour on stage. Following the Italian custom he selected or invented scenarios with an ancient historical background. But this background was a convention in no way disguising the contemporary attitudes his characters display. The theory that only kings and others of high birth were capable of exhibiting heroic behaviour to a supreme degree, coupled with the practical consideration that autocrats were opera's most powerful patrons, induced librettists such as Zeno to emphasise the virtuous qualities of their princely characters. These princes obeyed the moral code in all circumstances, and the conflicts that arose as a result of their adherence to it were considered the essence of tragedy. Sad endings to opera were not thought necessary or even appropriate in most cases.[2]

Various critical comparisons were made in the eighteenth century between the dramas of Corneille and Racine on the one hand and the librettos of Zeno and his younger and even more famous compatriot, Pietro Metastasio, on the other. Such comparisons show how highly these two librettists were esteemed. Indeed Metastasio was ranked among the greatest dramatists of all time and achieved an ascendency in the realm of libretto-writing that has hardly ever been equalled. It is significant that the work of the Italians should be linked with French spoken drama rather than French librettos, such as Quinault's, also influenced by Classicism. This is partly because both these Italian texts and French spoken drama excluded supernatural phenomena, dancing and divertissements.* Quinault's librettos conspicuously contained these very features.

The major, non-literary factor that Zeno, Metastasio and other librettists of Italian opera had to bear in mind was the musical aria. Ample provision had to be made for arias, with the occasional duet and ensemble, since these were what many in the audience came to hear. The policy librettists adopted was to write the greater part of a libretto as though it were a spoken drama—most of this could be set as recitative—but to insert at intervals short lyrical verses which would become the aria texts. The chief difficulty—

---

*We should note, however, that separately-devised ballets were permitted as entr'actes to *opera seria*.

one that increased for a time in the early eighteenth century—was to position these verses correctly.

Eighteenth-century *opera seria* was sung by star performers whose overbearing and pompous attitude has been made famous through B. Marcello's brilliant satire *Il teatro alla moda*, 1720.[3] Singers affected the plan of the libretto by being customarily allocated more or fewer arias as befitted their status. They had also become accustomed, by the beginning of the century, to retire from the stage after singing an aria. So the number and allocation of arias determined the majority of the singers' exits and therefore to some extent their entries and the whole dramatic plan.

The librettists' main concession to music therefore was the aria and the manipulation of the scenario around a given number of exits. Skill was required to make these seem natural rather than superimposed by the external circumstance of the singers' demands. Metastasio was particularly adept at writing and positioning an aria for each character in an act in turn, then—in Acts I and II— giving an extra aria at the end of the act to the two or three chief characters. In this way the singers' honour was satisfied, or almost. Carlo Goldoni, writing in his *Mémoires* published in 1787, tells the interesting anecdote of how his libretto *Amalasunta*, presented to a Milanese opera company in 1733, was refused primarily on the grounds that it transgressed certain conventions regarding the allocation of particular types of aria to particular singers. He was informed by one of the company's directors what these conventions were:

The three principal personages of the drama ought to sing five airs each; two in the first act, two in the second, and one in the third. The second actress and the second soprano can only have three, and the inferior characters must be satisfied with a single air each, or two at the most. The author of the words must furnish the musician with the different shades which form the *chiaroscuro* of music, and take care that two pathetic airs do not succeed one another. He must distribute with the same precaution the bravura airs, the airs of action, the inferior airs, and the minuets and the rondeaus.

He must, above all things, avoid giving impassioned airs, bravura airs, or rondeaus, to inferior characters; these poor devils must be satisfied with what they can get, and every opportunity of distinguishing themselves is denied them.[4]

This particular classification of arias should be accepted with caution, mainly because Goldoni talks of 'minuets' and 'rondeaus' which were not Italian aria forms of the 1730's. What emerges is the general principle that the librettist had to think in terms of a variety of musical styles and write his aria verses accordingly. Whether librettists or composers ever made any rigid classification of aria types is a moot point, though J. Brown, who made his own list of aria types in a little book that appeared in 1789, thought not:

> Whether the Italian composers, in observing these distinctions, have been guided by some system, or have been merely influenced by feeling, I cannot take it upon me to say. I am rather, however, inclined to think that the latter is the case; in the first place, because I never heard of any such system existing among them, and, because I have been personally acquainted with several of their finest composers now living, that had no idea of it; and again, because I think, that, to the want of such a system can be alone attributed the gross deviations . . . from its most obvious and most essential principles.[5]

An aria was supposed to be an emotional climax or summary of the previous scene but, having by Metastasio's time ceased to be actually part of the action, was really a contemplative or emotional 'afterthought' to it. This merely accentuated an already strong duality in Italian opera. *Opera seria* was considered both a literary and a musical form in which poetry and music came to the fore alternately. The theory behind this was expressed by Burney who, on his visit to Vienna in 1772, referred to Metastasian opera as

> the ancient form of the musical drama, in which the poet and musician claim equal attention from an audience; the bard in the recitatives and narrative parts; and the composer in the airs, duos and chorusses.[6]

We know that some audiences paid scant attention to the narrative recitative,* though they could and did study copies of the libretto in the theatre at their leisure. However, Burney's statement reveals Metastasio's beliefs that *opera seria* should be more than just musical entertainment and that the best policy was to confine lyrical and dramatic music to particular sections and not let it encroach on the literary preserve of the rest of the opera.

The carefully arranged balance between poetry and music was

*See p. 41.

most likely to be upset if musicians started to develop recitative and turn it into a lyrical and expressive medium. In practice they exerted themselves not at all in *secco* recitative, which retained its set and stereotyped formulas without change throughout the eighteenth century.[7] Recitative accompanied by the orchestra, however, was another matter. Composers came gradually to realise that here was a type of recitative with infinite possibilities, so the main eighteenth-century developments took place within it. These included long orchestral ritornellos and lyrical, arioso passages. The musical superiority of accompanied over *secco* recitative was unquestioned, partly because the weight and variety of orchestral tone could reinforce at any moment a section, a detail, of recitative text that required more expansive treatment or some particular emphasis. For this reason it obviously commended itself to musicians and, to some extent, to the public also.[8] Metastasio, however, maintained in a letter written in 1749 to the composer J. Hasse that the sound of the strings should not be 'rendered too familiar' in recitative. Giving advice about where accompanied recitatives might suitably be composed in a new setting of his libretto *Attilio Regolo*, Metastasio suggested four occasions, two in Act I and one each in Acts II and III.[9] Such advice was based partly on the observation that stringed accompaniments and ritornellos slowed down the pace of the dialogue. Accompanied recitative, therefore, was not recommended for passages where fast speech or action was required.

Alas, a concert-like succession of arias with intervening and sometimes very dull recitative builds neither a cogent nor very coherent music drama. It was nevertheless found tolerable by those many spectators who went to the theatre primarily for social reasons. For audiences that did not wish to pay perpetual attention to the action, *opera seria* was ideal. It contained enough good music and literature to please the patron with artistic sensibilities yet mixed them in a manner which also pleased the philistine. The audiences that encouraged a larger than average number of arias, accompanied recitatives, and choruses in their Italian operas were usually north-European. These seem to have made no pretence of caring for the rights of literature in opera and must often, because of their imperfect knowledge of the language, have remained unmoved by Metastasio's poetry. A letter from Giuseppe Riva, an Italian librettist working in England, dated 3 October 1726,

explains that Zeno's and Metastasio's librettos unaltered were not
acceptable to the London Royal Academy of Music where 'few
verses of recitative and many arias' were wanted.[10] All the Metastasian texts set by Handel for London productions were adapted.
Generally speaking, the demand outside Italy for a more musical
opera seria was to the better composers' advantage. It tended to
make them set proportionately longer sections of the opera with
skill and employ a larger variety of musical techniques and mediums.
As a result, many of what we would regard as the most successful
eighteenth-century Italian operas were written for London (by
Handel), for certain German courts and for the Russian court at
St Petersburg.

The public's musical taste was a comparatively known factor, and
composers had to write to suit the locality. There is no more
interesting illustration of this than the operas of the Neapolitan
composer Nicolò Piccinni, written for Paris between 1778 and 1787.
Brought from Naples to Paris to demonstrate the superiority of
the Italian style over Gluck's, Piccinni made a marked attempt to
alter details of his musical language to please French audiences.
Conversely, operas by different composers written for one type of
audience in one particular geographical area often show strong
resemblances. Individuality in music was less highly prized than its
up-to-dateness to suit the region. This is one reason why we can
often more easily tell the approximate date of composition of an
opera than the name of its composer. In Italy especially the pressure
on composers to keep their styles modern was intense. *Opera seria*
in Italy was not always the most satisfying kind of *opera seria*
dramatically, but it tended for a long time to be the stylistic pace-
maker for Italian opera abroad.

Another reason for the uniformity of style among Italian operas
of any one period was the common educational background of
many of the composers. Naples was the great Italian training centre
for eighteenth-century operatic musicians, and its conservatorios
attracted many young foreigners who in previous centuries would
have gone to Venice for their musical instruction. Italian opera of
the early and mid-eighteenth century has loosely been termed
'Neapolitan' mainly because so many of the composers of that
period emerged from Naples. The adjective is as suitable as any, if
one has to be found, though slightly confusing since it has been
applied to operas constructed on the strict, alternating recitative-

aria plan as well as to operas by eighteenth-century, Neapolitan-trained composers. The first meaning has slightly more universal applications than the second.

An analysis of early eighteenth-century *opera seria* is really one of individual items: recitatives, arias, duets, the occasional vocal ensemble and short chorus, and the instrumental overture. Of no other type of opera is it so true to say that the whole is merely the sum of its parts. The overture almost inevitably follows a fast-slow-fast, three-section formula. The arias, by far the largest and most important group of lyrical items, are almost inevitably in *da capo* form. Since no major difference of structure is to be sought between one aria and the next, what structural variations there are occur in the internal organisation of phrases and motives. Changes within *da capo* form over the period 1700–50 involve the development of a binary structure within the first (and last) section, also a growing inequality in length and musical value between the first and second sections—to the extent that the second finally seems little more than an interlude or connecting passage between the first section and its repeat. The imbalance was one reason why a breakaway from *da capo* form was ultimately desirable and why, c. 1760, there was a general move towards binary forms and towards free ternary forms with resemblances to the shape of sonata and concerto first movements of that period.[11] The Italians at home were the most conservative and retained the *da capo* convention longest.

The *da capo* structure was selected for the aria primarily for musical reasons, and all the evidence suggests that the aria verses were constructed to suit the form of the music rather than vice versa. The fact that arias were so consistently set in one and the same mould, whatever the sense of the words, implies a desire on the part of composers and others for clear, regular structures. Into this mould were poured various types of musical content inspired —at least in theory—by the 'affection' of the words, though the texts came to consist chiefly of generalised and philosophical maxims too ethereal for composers to 'imitate' in any obvious way. Gradually set apart from the drama, the aria became more and more pure music. Already by the 1680's–90's composers were setting words with more attention to their phonetic sounds than their meaning. Pleasant-sounding words and phrases were repeated many times in aria settings and themselves became part of the music. Vocalisations were placed on open vowel sounds not merely for expressive or pictorial reasons but also because of the actual beauty of the vowels:

Ex 10   *A. Scarlatti*, La Teodora augusta, *1693, I, vii*
(*MS Oxford, Christ Church 991*)

vi   le mie

pe - ne   lu - sin - ga - - - - - - -

- - - - - - - te

The long, drawn-out vocalisations tended to increase the purely 'instrumental' quality of the vocal line, and indeed the whole aria was becoming more instrumental in style. The increasing number of instrumental parts, the enlargement and growing number of orchestral ritornellos, the identical phraseology of passages for

voice and instruments, were all having their effect. For the first
time players were beginning to challenge the technical superiority
of vocalists, and a spirit of competition between them may be felt
in certain arias, especially at the turn of the seventeenth and beginning of the eighteenth centuries, where *obbligato* instruments play
or alternate with the voice. That Italian singers could more than
hold their own is shown by Burney's anecdote of the famous
castrato Farinelli who, during the performance of a particular aria,
had a musical duel with a trumpeter in the orchestra. The two
together performed a vocalisation—or cadenza, it is not clear which
from Burney's account—which they largely contrived on the spot
and in which each tried to outdo the other.[12] Farinelli is reported to
have won outright.

Technical virtuosity is not the only sign of concerto influence
upon the aria. Most arias by composers like Alessandro Scarlatti
and Handel contain semi-polyphonic part-writing and some of their
arias include contrapuntal devices. Concertos by early eighteenth-
century composers such as Albinoni and Vivaldi, however, show
leanings towards a more homophonic style with the top orchestral
and solo parts receiving all the melodic and virtuoso material and
the lower orchestral parts just the harmonic and rhythmic sub-
structure. This strong contrast between melodic and supporting
parts soon characterises the aria too. Some of Vivaldi's own arias
show the tendency.

Ex 11   *Vivaldi*, Armida al campo d'Egito, *1718, III, v*
                          (MS Turin, Bibl. Naz. Foa 38 (1))

OSMIRA

Se cor- rendo in se-no al mare

A comparison of Examples 10 and 11 shows the sort of stylistic change taking place over the period 1690–1720, and above all the growing discrepancy between melody and accompaniment. In Example 11 the lower orchestral parts have a totally subordinate function. The even quavers of Vivaldi's bass line are a typical feature of many an aria of the 1720's—a period when in Italy polyphonic idioms were generally going out of fashion—and have the one virtue of providing an illusion of pace in allegro movements even where the rate of harmonic change is a slow one. Quite distinct from the bass, the violin line of Example 11 shows signs of that over-fussy decoration which got worse for a time in the mid-eighteenth century as performing techniques improved. Fast scales, acciaccaturas, trills of various kinds, became too often an end in themselves and blurred the outline of what might otherwise have been pleasing melodies.

The increased emphasis on melody and its ornamentation was not quite sufficient to make up for the loss of expression caused by the dismissal of counterpoint, so that extra technical aids to expression were necessary. Dynamic markings are not at all unknown in seventeenth-century scores, though they become much more common in those of the next century. The term 'crescendo' appears it is—believed for the first time—in the score of *Artaserse* by Nicola Jommelli, 1749,[13] but the practice of applying crescendos and decrescendos in performance was certainly in general use before that date. De Brosses, on his visit to Rome in 1740, declared that the opera orchestras there were in the habit of swelling and diminishing their tone.[14] In the scores of some arias the crescendo is denoted by the term *rinforzando* or by a graded series of *p, mp, mf, f* signs. In others the crescendo seems implied by the nature of the music itself, especially where, as in the example below dating from 1753, the opening bars rise to an unmistakable climax:

Ex 12   *Jommelli*, Attilio Regolo, *1753, II, ii*
                              (*MS Cambridge, Fitzwilliam Mus. 22 F 2*)

continued/

va – da   il   pie non o – – sa   nò

non o – – sa   che   vi –

Another and very prominent innovation in *opera seria* of the 1740's–50's is the type of orchestral legato-staccato contrast demonstrated in the music above. Staccato techniques almost certainly found their way in by way of *opera buffa*; but whereas there they had dramatic and comic value, in *opera seria* they became more abstract in their effect and association. They intrigued the ear and reinforced that sense of rather jittery excitement that composers of the mid-century tried so often to create. The trouble was that the many sharp contrasts fashionable at that period were employed too indiscriminately in too many places. Greater extremes of contrast could hardly be found and some reaction in favour of simpler musical styles was soon inevitable.

The 1760's is a period when the music of *opera seria* shows distinct signs of flagging inspiration. Very noticeable is the contraction in the number of musical idioms employed. A study of Mozart's *Mitridate Re di Ponto* will reveal the severely limited, hedged-in styles common in *opera seria* of the year 1770. Mozart was far too young at that time—he was only fourteen—to do more than parody current musical conventions, but he did it well enough to receive approbation and other commissions. The basic trouble was that neither the composers nor the public believed any longer in the sentiments expressed in Zeno's and Metastasio's dramas. The heroic actions of Metastasio's characters now appeared old-fashioned and lacking in contemporary relevance.

In order to understand this stylistic contraction further, we should bear in mind the court fashions *opera seria* reflected. The more exclusively composers and singers strove to please the aristocrat and cultured man of leisure, the wider grew the gap between the music of *opera seria* and folk and street song. Seventeenth-century Venetian opera had been much more closely allied to folksong and dance. Lilting $\frac{6}{8}$ and $\frac{12}{8}$ rhythms with particular folksong or dance associations were still common in *opere serie* at the beginning of the eighteenth century—as those by A. Scarlatti testify—but later tended to disappear altogether from this kind of work. A possible deduction from the fact that these styles continued exclusively for a while in comic opera is that composers were now mindful of the propriety of particular sorts of music, and that definite 'heroic' and 'comic' styles were beginning to form. The development brought a bigger stylistic contraction to *opera seria* than to *opera buffa*. Mid-century composers always felt able to parody 'heroic'

styles for the sake of comedy but became temporarily reluctant to
enliven a tragic text with music that was at all like popular song.

Heroic operas by Handel and other composers working in
Germany and England sometimes show conservative influences.
When Handel first arrived in England in 1710, after experience in
Hamburg and Italy, his style was Italianate and modern. But his
long residence in England, plus the fact that English audiences were
not so anxious for musical change as the Italians, permitted him to
adhere to idioms which gradually become more and more dated by
Italian standards. Frederick the Great wrote in 1737, when he was
still heir apparent to the throne: 'Handel's great days are over, his
inspiration is exhausted and his taste behind the fashion'.[15] Nowadays we may prefer Handel's old-fashioned taste to Frederick's.
Handel's operas of the 1720's–30's contain more stylistic variety
than the work of contemporary composers keeping strictly to the
modern idiom.

Handel never forgot his younger days in Hamburg where *da
capo* form had been far from obligatory and where *ariosos*, songs
and instrumental sections had been used to create much freer over-
all structures than were possible in the Metastasian type of opera.
The relatively free forms of much of his *Orlando furioso*, 1733, with
its many *ariosos*, reflect the music of the Hamburg operas with
which Handel was earlier acquainted. He was lucky in the sense
that he could always revert to earlier methods whenever he found
the *secco* recitative and *da capo* formula too strict and uncompromis-
ing. Composers writing for the first time in the middle of the
century began with the quite different background of Metastasian
opera. Handel was fortunate, too, in having experience of opera
in Germany, where the standard of wind playing was high and
where wind instruments were generally used with more understanding and daring than in Italy. The same sort of understanding
is shown in his operas written for London.

We may deduce that London audiences were less insistent on
musical novelty than their Italian contemporaries from Handel's
policy of putting into production operas he had written ten or
even twenty years before. Although alterations were made for these
repeat productions, much of the music remained unchanged.
Repeat productions were also common in early eighteenth-century
Hamburg where Reinhard Keiser was the chief composer. While
both Handel and Keiser were content to learn certain techniques

from younger Italians, neither wished entirely to relinquish the semi-polyphonic idioms they had originally imbibed. Their reluctance to follow the ultra-modern trend without reserve was shared by other Germans who thought the kind of music in Example 11 (p. 116–17) too slick and empty in expression. Some of them were critical of Italian musical education. When the young composer Giuseppe Bonno returned to the Austrian imperial court from Naples, where he had received training, he was adjudged to have been insufficiently taught in counterpoint.[16] Johann Quantz, the famous German flute player, expressed what was probably the view of many, that Italian composers accepted too little technical instruction before launching forth on their own.[17]

Changes in the style and form of Italian opera abroad were often a direct reflection of patrons', and in some cases the autocrat's, personal taste. Frederick the Great—who was in a position to impose what changes he wanted at the Berlin opera—reached the conclusion that the form of the *da capo* aria was incongruous, chiefly because it led to too many repetitions of certain words. In *Montezuma*, 1755, set to music by his court composer Carl Heinrich Graun, we find his new predilection for 'cavatinas': songs similar in form and length to the first section of *da capo* arias.[18] In other mid-century courts the influence of *tragédie lyrique* made itself felt, nowhere more so than at Parma. The Infante Philip of Spain, awarded Parma by the treaty of Aix-la-Chapelle in 1748, was brought up in a French cultural atmosphere and appointed a Frenchman, du Tillot, to run the artistic affairs of his state. Du Tillot was much concerned with turning Parma into an artistic centre of the Enlightenment. Having first tried unsuccessfully to please the court with performances of French operas, he then thought of bringing together an Italian team to present operas in Italian but akin to Rameau's *tragédies lyriques* in form and spirit. The court librettist Carlo Frugoni, much influenced by Algarotti's recently published *Essay on the opera*,[19] cooperated with the composer Tommaso Traetta in two works, *Ippolito e Aricia*, 1759, and *I Tindaridi*, 1760, closely modelled on Rameau's *Hippolyte et Aricie* and *Castor et Pollux* respectively. These Traetta operas seem an odd cross between the, until then, totally contrasting genres of French and Italian heroic opera. The music is predominantly Italian but the textual framework is French in origin. These two works demonstrate that the most obvious method of revitalising *opera seria*, and one which recommended itself to operatic reformers, was to borrow the French dramatic system. This was precisely what Gluck did very shortly afterwards.

One of the strange paradoxes of this situation was that *opera buffa* was just then making a big impact in France, particularly on *opéra-comique*; so French and Italian opera were now mutually interacting. Comic opera was also affecting *opera seria* in a few localities, though in so gradual and unpremeditated a manner that this development went largely unpublicised and received less comment than the Parma experiment or Gluck's reform operas in Vienna. The influence of comic opera may be traced both in the gradually increasing number of duets and ensembles—some in a free form reminiscent of comic finales in *opera buffa*—and in the trend towards gayer and simpler melodic styles. An interesting mixture of 'heroic' and 'comic' music is found in Thomas Arne's *Artaxerses*, 1762, which contains lighthearted songs like those partially quoted below. This work is perhaps not entirely typical of its period, being an attempt at Italian-style heroic opera with English words. Nevertheless here are the signs of the 'popular' path along which heroic opera of the Italian kind was beginning to move:

Ex 13   *Extracts from T. Arne,* Artaxerses, *1762*
                                      (Publ. John Johnson, London)

Fair Se- mi - ra love - ly maid

cease in pi - ty to ___ up - braid ___

my op - press'd but ___ con - stant heart ___

continued/

1   G. M. Crescimbeni, *Storia dell'accademia degli Arcadi*, reprint, London, 1804, p. 5.

2   M. Fehr, *A. Zeno und seine Reform des Operntextes*, Zürich, 1912, pp. 73–4.

3   cf. O. Strunk, *Source readings in music history*, London, 1952, pp. 518 ff.

4   C. Goldoni, *Memoirs*, English edn, London, 1814, i, 185–6.

5   J. Brown, *Letters upon the poetry and music of the Italian opera*, Edinburgh 1789, pp. 41–2.

6   *Dr Burney's musical tours in Europe*, ed. Scholes, London, 1959, ii, 81.

7   cf. E. O. D. Downes, 'Secco recitative in early classical opera seria', *Journal of the American musicological society* xiv (1961), 64 ff.

8   G. Coyer, *Voyages d'Italie et de Hollande*, Paris, 1775, i, 192.

9   C. Burney, *Memoirs of the life and writings of the Abate Metastasio*, London, 1796, i, 321 ff.

10 O. E. Deutsch, *Handel, a documentary biography*, London, 1955, p. 197.

11 M. F. Robinson, 'The aria in opera seria, 1725–80', *Proceedings of the Royal Musical Association* lxxxviii (1961–2), 40–2.

12 *Dr Burney's musical tours*, i, 153.

13 H. Abert, *Niccolo Jommelli als Opernkomponist*, Halle, 1908, p. 215.

14 C. de Brosses, *Lettres familières écrites d'Italie en 1739 et 1740*, Paris, 1858, ii, 379.

15 Deutsch, op. cit., p. 441.

16 E. Wellesz, 'Giuseppe Bonno (1710–88). Sein Leben und seine dramatischen Werke', *Sammelbände der internationalen Musikgesellschaft* xi (1909–10), 438.

17 J. J. Quantz, *Versuch einer Anweisung die Flöte traversiere zu spielen*, ed. Schering, Leipzig, 1906, p. 9.

18 cf. the printed score in *Denkmäler Deutscher Tonkunst*, vol. XV, 1904.

19 E. Wellesz, 'Francesco Algarotti und seine Stellung zur Musik', *Sammelbände der internationalen Musikgesellschaft* xv (1913–14), 429–31.

9

COMIC OPERA

In chapter 3 we briefly mentioned some of the comic features of Venetian opera: the farcical situations involving the chief, high-ranking characters whose actions hardly seem compatible with their status, and the coarse wit and antics of the servants. Wrapped up in the form of a historical drama and mixed with heroic allusions, this comedy sometimes appears more serious than it is. But not all Italian comic operas of the period were of this type. A few were modern comedies with a rustic or town setting, and these made no pretensions whatever to being heroic drama. Their non-heroic qualities are emphasised by the characters involved: small landed or town gentry with their families and servants, also various professional men such as lawyers, tutors or soldiers. These and other characters tend to become stock figures in Italian comic opera as they had been in classical and Renaissance comedies. The various innocent mistakes —frequently confusions of personal identity—and guileful deceptions—especially by the young on the old—form the basis of the scenario and provide a further link with comedies of the past. The street and market scenes that sometimes occur are also a traditional feature and become, especially in eighteenth-century comic operas, a valuable means of fixing the locality of the story. The servants sometimes speak dialect, which may also serve to give a specifically local flavour to the work.

In the earliest comic operas parody comes clearly to the fore. One target was the supernatural element of early Venetian opera and its various gods and allegorical figures. By arranging the appearance of a false deity—manufactured with the aid of wires and appliances by

E

one character in the story as a trick on the rest—the librettist could
humorously expose the unreal nature of all such supernatural
visitations in opera.[1] So the chief schemer in *Il potestà di Colognole*,
words by G. A. Moniglia and music by J. Melani, 1657, contrives
the appearance of four furies who suddenly, at the end of Act II,
rush through the air and create panic among the characters present.
In Act III the same character tries another trick of summoning a
false devil—a specific parody, so it has been suggested, of Medea's
summoning of the furies in Act I of Cavalli's *Giasone*, 1649.[2]

The earliest comic operas with a modern setting were promoted
and patronised primarily by the upper classes. *Che soffre, speri*, 1639,
and *Dal male il bene*, 1653, were performed under the auspices of
the influential Barberini family at Rome and had librettos by
Giulio Rospigliosi, later Pope Clement IX. *Il potestà* was the
inaugural work at the Pergola theatre in Florence before an audience
that included a cardinal. Even in the eighteenth century the Italian
aristocracy never completely lost interest in comic opera, though
the counter-attraction and exclusiveness of *opera seria* tended for a
while at least to draw its allegiance. The growth of *opera seria*,
however, was no disaster for comic opera, for the non-aristocratic
classes were by this time beginning to evince such enthusiasm for it
that in certain cases they supported it largely on their own. Generally speaking, the early eighteenth century shows many signs of a
reaction against the exclusiveness of opera of the establishment.

The form and results of the reaction varied from place to place.
In Italian centres such as Venice the desire for comedy in opera
found its commonest expression through the *intermezzo*, an
entr'acte or group of two, occasionally three, entr'actes, which
was performed with *opera seria* but was nevertheless distinct from
it. These intermezzos were descended from the various comic
scenes for the servants in Venetian opera, scenes which, once moved
to the ends of acts, effectively became entr'actes and quite independent of the parent work. Thus they often came to be written
by different people from those responsible for the *opera seria*. They
finally grew to short, two-scene comic operas that could be performed, quite separately from the operas they originally accompanied, on their own or with other intermezzos or with spoken
plays to fill out an evening's entertainment.

Another, and perhaps even more important, result was the
beginning, in 1709, of the first regular season of comic operas in

Naples.[3] Up to that time comic operas in a modern setting and with
bourgeois characters had been produced but sporadically in Italy.
In 1709 one of the two Neapolitan opera houses, the Fiorentini,
was in danger of closing down for lack of support. The impresarios
of the theatre then thought of certain comic operas in dialect that
had been previously performed in Neapolitan private circles and
decided to try similar works on the public stage. The venture was
an immediate success and the Fiorentini became a recognised locale
for *opera buffa*. These early Neapolitan works have a distinct flavour
of their own, the majority being wholly or partly in Neapolitan
dialect and with scenes reflecting the everyday life in the streets of
the locality. The dialect may have been one reason for the fact
that these works did not become popular in other parts of Italy.
Other Italian towns preferred to wait a few years before they too
ran regular seasons of comic operas. Their operas were seldom in
dialect, a factor which often contributed to their success outside the
area of origin. The intermezzos which accompanied *opera seria* in the
élite Neapolitan opera house shared the same distinction of not being
in dialect. Some of these Neapolitan intermezzos—especially the
most famous of all, Pergolesi's *La serva padrona*, 1733—received
international acclaim. Pergolesi's *opere buffe* with roles in dialect, on
the other hand, were successful at home but unperformed elsewhere.

After Lully's death his successors at the *Académie* in Paris were in
the position to decide when and in what form comedy could appear
in French opera. In fact, comic opera appeared sporadically on the
Académie's boards and the influences working towards regular
seasons of comic opera in France came largely from outside the
Académie altogether. The story of the birth of *opéra-comique* is one
involving long legal struggles between various official and unofficial theatrical organisations. Of the official groups the *Comédie
française* and the *Comédie italienne* were concerned as much as the
Académie. The granting of the patent to Lully in 1672 meant that
other acting troupes were limited in the number of singers and
instrumentalists they might employ and were banned from producing works with continuous music. The severe limitations on
their musical resources brought protests at the time and later led
some organisations to challenge the patent, not openly but by
surreptitious methods: gradually adding extra musicians and
musical items to their shows until such time as the *Académie* clamped
down. Among the non-privileged troupes with few rights under

the law were those performing at the Parisian fairgrounds of St
Germain and St Laurent. These were not likely to excite the wrath
of the officially constituted bodies so long as they confined themselves to acrobatic and juggling displays or to marionette shows.
Their moves towards presenting plays and revues of better quality
at the turn of the seventeenth century and beyond, however, were
an infringement of privilege and challenged by the *Comédie
française* which attempted to confine them once more to a
thoroughly subordinate position.[4] That the *Comédie* was unsuccess-
ful in the long run was because of the extraordinary ingenuity of the
fair managers at finding new and technically legal methods of
theatrical presentation. When they were forbidden to act all
'comédie, colloque ou dialogue' in 1706, 'pièces en monologues'
were introduced. When even these were stopped, and the fair
actors effectively forbidden to speak, the customary habit of
French audiences of singing in opera and other musical shows came
to their aid. Audiences were invited to enliven the performance by
singing to popular tunes of the day verses hung on large boards
above the stage. The actors meanwhile mimed their parts. Here for
the first time music played a decisive part in the survival of what we
now know as *opéra-comique*.

   The popular tunes that found their way into *opéra-comique* were
known as *vaudevilles*, one writer defining these as 'des chansons,
souvent fort anciennes, dont l'air original, devenu populaire, peut
être appliqué à d'autres paroles'.[5] Such tunes, taken from all kinds
of sources including operas by Lully, Rameau and others, were
each designated by a *timbre* or short title printed in the libretto above
the verse the tune was to accompany. The importance of these
vaudevilles is further demonstrated in the next part of the story, as
recounted by the French dramatist Le Sage:

   Les Forains, voyant que le public goûtoit ce spectacle en chansons,
   s'imaginèrent avec raison que si les Acteurs chantoient eux-mêmes les
   vaudevilles, ils plairoient encore davantage. Ils traitèrent alors avec l'Opéra
   qui en vertu de ses patentes, leur accorda la permission de chanter. On
   composa aussitôt des pièces purement en vaudevilles et le spectacle prit le
   nom d'*Opéra Comique*. On mêla peu à peu de la prose avec les vers pour
   mieux lier les couplets ou pour se dispenser d'en trop faire de communs:
   de sorte qu'insensiblement les pièces devinrent mixtes.[6]

In fact, neither the term *opéra-comique* nor the use of vaudevilles was new. The new accord of the fair theatres with the *Académie*, however, meant that the term had official sanction and the show had officially recognised features of its own. The *Académie* would probably never have made the agreement had its own finances been in perfect order, but its managers very likely argued that an extra financial inflow—and indirectly a greater financial and controlling interest in the fair shows—was to their advantage. However, they were not prepared to see jeopardised the unique features of opera at the *Académie* and were particularly firm on preventing any substitution, in *opéra-comique*, of spoken dialogue by recitative. The point was that recitative would be the most vital step forward to an *opéra-comique* with original, through-composed music, and when recitative did appear in a few such operas in the 1750's the *Académie* saw to it that there was no reoccurrence.

Opéra-comique between 1720 and 1750 might have a continuous chain of vaudevilles or else alternating spoken dialogue and songs which included vaudevilles and, often, original and more sophisticated music. However, since the musical bias at first leaned towards tunes already well known, the composer's role was not so important here as in other contemporary types of opera in France or Italy. Because *opéra-comique* derived from plays with music rather than from opera, the librettists were the key men in its earlier days and the composers generally men of lesser significance.

Likewise the man most often associated with the English *Beggar's Opera*, 1728, is John Gay, its librettist, not John Pepusch, the composer who arranged its music. This most famous of English ballad operas makes an obvious comparison with *opéra-comique*. Once again dialogue and songs alternate, the tunes selected from various song-books in circulation at the time and therefore already well known. The tunes chosen form a most heterogeneous collection, some originating in the sixteenth century and possibly earlier, others relatively modern. Many were from British sources but others—perhaps significantly in view of the parallel with *opéra-comique*—were French. In addition to folksongs, there were tunes by famous composers including Handel (the march from *Rinaldo*) and Purcell (two airs, one each from *Dioclesian* and *The Fairy Queen*). The main task for Pepusch, one of the many German musicians who came over to England in the early eighteenth century, was the composition of an overture and the *basso continuo* accompaniments to the various songs. Commentators have suggested that he had little or no say in the selection of the tunes.[7]

The Beggar's Opera is both a satire on the graft and corruption found in Gay's England and a tilt, as the introduction makes plain, at the Italian opera in London. In the introduction is the interesting sentence: 'I hope I may be forgiven, that I have not made my opera throughout unnatural like those in vogue; for I have no recitative.' The remark suggests that the old prejudice against recitative had not entirely disappeared. It is possible to assume that this dislike contributed to the form of English ballad opera in the eighteenth century with its airs and spoken dialogue. Although *The Beggar's Opera* by no means caused the death of Italian opera in England, as has sometimes been suggested, it was a contributory factor in the closure of the London Royal Academy of Music, which had been responsible for Italian opera in London between 1719 and 1728. Unlike *opéra-comique* in France, *The Beggar's Opera*, with other ballad operas of the period, was competing with heroic opera in a foreign language. It may therefore be considered an expression of that patriotic dislike that was undoubtedly felt for the imported opera with its *castrati* and *prime donne*. Likewise comic opera in the vernacular and with spoken dialogue (*Singspiel*) became popular in Germany in the mid-eighteenth century, partly because it catered for a taste that preferred local opera, however rough and ready, to opera expertly done but under Italian guidance.

Although the various comic opera movements began as a reaction against heroic opera, each was in a way complementary to the heroic opera in its particular country. This shows itself in various features: for instance, the element of the miraculous entered scenarios of early *opéra-comique* (shades here of *tragédie lyrique*) but not of early *opera buffa*, which was affected by *opera seria*. More important, the qualities of heroic opera, plus the claims to supremacy made on its behalf, were a definite incentive to the creators of comic opera to do better. They raised standards by direct parody and by concentrating on better drama. This in turn led to a gradual change in the quality of the comedy presented.

It was relatively easy to write a comic opera or intermezzo consisting of a series of witty puns, slapstick, and practical jokes; easy also, and the ethics of the time saw no harm in this, to draw laughter at the expense of personal ugliness or old age, or some uncouth idiosyncrasy such as a stutter. The more deformed, senile or foolish the character, the better he could be derided in both words

and music. Rameau's *comédie lyrique*, *Platée*, 1745, is a good example
of this slightly unpleasant humour.[8] It was less easy to portray
characters in depth and present both tricksters and fooled as human
beings with variable and even likable qualities. That a more humane
type of comedy gradually entered opera is due partly to changing
social attitudes in the eighteenth century, and partly to the influence of certain librettists, Carlo Goldoni being outstanding, who
realised that wit was superior to clownery.

Features of Italian *opera buffa* affecting the quality of its comedy
included *parti serie*, characters with 'serious' or semi-heroic qualities,
who appeared alongside the *parti buffe*, the comic characters. These
two groups were in about equal numbers. The *parti serie* were
'respectable' representatives of the middle class or possibly of the
lower orders of the aristocracy. Their respectability by comparison
with the others—the stock figures referred to earlier*—shows itself
in their parodying of *opera seria*: their tendency to leave the stage
after an aria, their refined feelings and speech (never in dialect),
and their aloofness from the clownish antics of their fellows. In
early eighteenth-century *opera buffa* at Naples, in which this strong
distinction between *parti serie* and *buffe* first clearly appears, the two
groups are so set apart that separate actions tend to form, one carried
forward by each. The rigidness of this handling suggests that
Neapolitan librettists had at first little idea how to fuse serious
elements with comedy but were nevertheless prompted to attempt
it to give a more elevated tone to their work.[9]

The problem of writing a satisfactory scenario with two such
groups of characters was not eased by other factors closely involving
the music. In seventeenth-century opera the Italians had already
introduced vocal ensembles at the end of a comic act or scene,
ensembles in which the characters are in conflict and lampooning,
threatening, or arguing with, each other.[10] Although no one
objected to comedians singing against each other, there were
objections to the serious characters doing likewise, since these
would then be seen in an 'unnatural' and ridiculous light foreign to
their supposed true nature. In order to write the sort of boisterous
comic finale which became the convention, early eighteenth-
century librettists had in practice to remove their serious characters
from the stage and introduce their comedians for the act endings.
In the case of the last act, Act III, a different convention applied.

*See p. 129.

Everyone was customarily on stage at the end of the work and the ensemble here could not be a comic finale because of the presence of the serious characters. Instead, this ensemble was a rather tame affair, the action having finished before it began and everyone singing in harmonious and unruffled accord.

Goldoni and other mid-century librettists increased the proportion of *parti buffe* to *parti serie* so that at last a majority of the characters could take part in one consolidated action. These librettists also introduced a limited number of *mezzi caratteri*, characters with neutral, and therefore rather colourless, qualities, who could combine with either group. These *mezzi caratteri* were a sign of a relaxation in the rather rigid rules of character portrayal, and were musically important because they could sing in comic ensembles, swelling the number of participants and therefore the varieties of vocal texture. Finally, *c.* 1770, serious characters also began to enter comic ensembles and finales, a further significant advance. The extent of this advance is at once clear if we reflect on the possible loss had Mozart not been able to write ensembles in which Donna Anna and Donna Elvira sang with Leporello and Zerlina. Put to act and sing simultaneously, these different types of character often disclose new and interesting facets of personality. This is particularly true of the normally respectable characters who, suddenly entering into the spirit of an ensemble and perhaps engaging in a dispute or prank, thus reveal a side to their nature not hitherto suspected.

The decision by da Ponte and Mozart to use the rather sensational story of Don Giovanni for an opera is symptomatic of developments in all forms of comic opera in the late eighteenth century. Scenarios are now much more harrowing and pathetic, relying less and less on pure comedy. Threats against the lives and honour of the innocent, tearful separations between lovers, clashes between the law and the outlaw, are now to be classed among its common themes. Of outside influences novels by Prévost, Richardson, Fielding, etc., are important, affecting not merely the plots but also the 'romantic' settings now appearing—Turkish harems, deserts, caverns, old and decaying castles, ballrooms, and country villages and inns.

Opera buffa could not have developed as it did without the aid of new, subtle forms of musical humour. The more grotesque methods of raising a laugh through music were the easiest and longest established. It was easy to put a character in a faintly ridiculous

light by having him deliver a fast, non-stop flow of words, the
sort of jabber we find in Don Bartolo's aria 'La vendetta' from
Figaro and in countless earlier operas. Other devices to sharpen
ridicule included short, disconnected phrases and wide leaps in the
vocal line. Bass singers, who customarily acted the aged male
roles, were often given such wide ranges that their top notes
were probably sung falsetto. The same sort of device, however, was
not so suited to portray the younger comic characters, traditionally
more sprightly and cleverer than their elders; and for a while during
the baroque period composers could only provide them with music
in the lighter and more popular idioms generally available at the
time. One of the chief musical advances made by Neapolitan
composers of the 1720's–30's, of whom Giovanni Battista Pergolesi
is the best known, was the invention of a tender and pathetic type
of melody which ideally personified the cajolery and wiles of the
young soubrette:

Ex 14   P. Auletta, La locandiera, *1738*, I, xii
        (MS Naples, Conservatorio S. Pietro a Maiella 24 5 20)

continued/

The short phrases, detached syllables, the constant feminine cadences, help to give this music a heart-rending quality new in opera. At the same time the characterisation of the young girl was not complete without some demonstration of her customary vivaciousness. In Serpina's aria 'A Serpina penserete' from Pergolesi's *La serva padrona* we see her two sides, her semi-seriousness and vivacity, in alternating $\frac{4}{4}$ (Largo) and $\frac{3}{8}$ (Allegro) sections. Serpina is here like the best of clowns, crying at one moment and laughing the next. The music deserves study for here is no single-sided presentation but characterisation in depth. It has a psychological acuteness beyond that found in most arias from *opera seria*.

Serpina acts as she sings and her music is not divorced from gesture and mime as many an aria in *opera seria* is. Although *opera seria* influence led early eighteenth-century composers to write the majority of their comic arias in *da capo* form (this was out of fashion by the end of the 1750's; from then on the freer forms of *opera buffa* tended to influence *opera seria*), the close alliance of music and action saved *opera buffa* from becoming totally conventionalised in its musical procedures. Among the items which most depended on the acting ability of the singers were the ensembles at the act endings. These were pieces in which composers could experiment with whatever kind of musical structure seemed suitable. In the earlier part of the eighteenth century ensembles were relatively short and sung by two or three singers who stayed on stage throughout. As long as this was so, the music could sometimes be made, if necessary, to fit some preconceived or abstract form. By the 1750's, however, these ensembles were embracing longer sections of the action, including moments of characters' entries and exits. Any straitjacketing of the music into a preconceived form was now finally out of the question.

A growing understanding of tonality was one of the chief factors that enabled eighteenth-century composers to expand the length of their ensembles. The longer the item, the more times the tonality was simply made to pass to and fro between tonic and related keys. Once composers were sure that a balanced key structure provided a flexible yet coherent underlay, they seemed less preoccupied with moving quickly from key to key. They now took their time to modulate, drew out the distance between cadences and held longer on to pedal points.

In the middle of the century Baldassare Galuppi, Nicolò Piccinni, and other opera composers began regularly to divide their longer ensembles into sections, each with its own time signature and speed. There had been previous attempts in this direction, though the full implications of what could be gained thereby had not been realised. The point was that as soon as the ensemble was no longer tied to one tempo, any number of sections could be added as the dramatic situation demanded. Composers did not need much intelligence to realise that the last section should have a fast tempo so that the music might gain excitement and momentum at the end. Dramatic insight, however, was required to determine where the changes in style and tempo should occur, also what the important moments were that needed emphasising. Since the ensemble was gradually getting longer and longer, it was in fact embracing much of the action that would, at an earlier period, have been set as *secco* recitative. The composer now had to control more precisely than before the pace, pauses, and emotional qualities of long stretches of the drama.

We can see an instance of a composer's perfect attention to dramatic detail if we look at the phrase:

Ex 15

Su - san - na!

sung by the Countess in the Act II finale of Mozart's *Nozze di Figaro*. The moment is the one where the Count, suspecting Cherubino to be clandestinely hidden in his wife's chamber, is surprised to find not Cherubino but Susanna inside. The Countess, with guilty feelings since she saw Cherubino enter, is as astonished to see her as the Count is. Her phrase gives the impression both of incredulous surprise and of secret relief. The music reflects the intense astonishment of all present (save Susanna) by a pause in which everything comes to a halt. Then, because the appearance of Susanna has quite altered the situation, the music changes to a new style. The impact of her appearance would have been spoiled had Mozart elected to keep his orchestra playing without a pause throughout the incident or chosen the point of change to a new section at a slightly different spot. Few composers—so a study of their scores suggests—had Mozart's ability to highlight such an incident in so telling a fashion.

It is interesting that such advances in musical dramatisation should take place in a genre which, not so very long before in the eighteenth century, had been considered very inferior drama by intellectuals and persons of quality. Until the courts stepped in with their patronage, *opera buffa* productions were often dowdy affairs as regards costumes and scenery; the singing too was of recognisably lower standard than that in *opera seria*. But, according to at least one perceptive commentator, the limited vocal techniques of the actors were a help, not a hindrance, to the development of *opera buffa*. Because its arias were rarely an excuse for vocal display, because its tunes were undoubtedly simpler and more popular than the tunes of *opera seria* and, we surmise, not so embellished in performance, there was a more heartfelt quality about its music in general. Algarotti writes in his *Essay*:

It must not, however, be hence concluded, that no vestige of true music is to be perceived among us; because, as a proof against such an opinion, and that no small one, may be produced our intermezzi, and comic Operas, wherein the first of all musical requisites, that of expression, takes the lead more than in any other of our compositions: which is owing perhaps to the impossibility the masters found of indulging their own fancy in a wanton display of all the secrets of their art, and the manifold treasures of musical knowledge; from which ostentatious prodigality, they were luckily prevented by the very limited abilities of their singers.[11]

These 'limited abilities' obviously did not include a lack of musicality. Thomas Gray, writing in 1763 to Algarotti after reading his *Essay*, has this to say:

I cannot help telling you, that 8 or 10 years ago, I was a witness of the power of your comic musick. There was a little troop of Buffi, that exhibited a Burletta in London, not in the Opera-House, where the audience is chiefly of the better sort, but in one of the common theatres full of all kinds of people & (I believe) the fuller from that natural aversion we bear to Foreigners: their looks & their noise made it evident, they did not come thither to hear; & on similar occasions I have known candles lighted, broken bottles, & penknives flung on the stage, the benches torn up, the scenes hurried into the street & set on fire. The curtains drew up, the musick was of Cocchi with a few airs of Pergolesi interspersed. The Singers were (as usual) deplorable, but there was one Girl (she call'd herself the Niccolina) with little voice & less beauty; but with the utmost justness of ear, the strongest expression of countenance, the most speaking eyes, the greatest vivacity & variety of gesture. Her first appearance instantly fix'd their attention; the tumult sunk at once, or if any murmur rose, it was soon hush'd by a general cry for silence. Her first air ravish'd every body; they forgot their prejudices, they forgot, that they did not understand a word of the language; they enter'd into all the humour of the part, made her repeat all her songs, & continued their transports, their laughter, & applause to the end of the piece.[12]

The mid-eighteenth century was a great period for small, travelling opera companies which performed in halls, palaces, theatres, wherever they could get a hearing. Of these the Italian troupes, like the one Gray describes that came to London, did a good service in bringing intermezzos and short *opere buffe* to the attention of the general public abroad. In August 1752 one Italian troupe achieved the great distinction of performing on the stage of the *Académie royale* in Paris, and remained in the city two years. Among the pieces in its repertoire was Pergolesi's *La serva padrona*, which had previously been performed in 1746 at the *Comédie italienne* and had made little impression.[13] Quite different was the effect of this work now. By performing on the stage of what was the traditional home of French opera, the Italians were bound to show French audiences quite unequivocally how different Italian opera was from their own. The managers of the *Académie* probably guessed their invitation to the Italians would raise controversy, both because there had been disputes in the past over which of the two nations produced the best opera and because recent pamphlets and articles had shown the existence in France of groups of intellectuals, including Rousseau and Grimm, who might form the nucleus of a pro-Italian faction.[14] Nevertheless, the eighteenth-century mentality was not such as would shirk controversy, and crowds could be expected to go to an opera over which there was some dispute as they would to a bear fight. It was improbable, however, that anyone foresaw the full repercussions of the visitors' appearance. Their performance quickly raised such argument that pro-French and pro-Italian factions formed to fight a pamphlet war (the so-called *Guerre des Bouffons*) in which court politics became involved. Rousseau writes in his *Confessions* about the troupe and the effect it had:

Although they were execrable and the orchestra—at that time a most ignorant lot—performed wilful murder on the pieces they played, the Italians did not fail to do irreparable damage to French Opera. The comparison between the two idioms, which could be heard on the same day and in the same theatre, opened French ears; absolutely no one could endure their drawling music after the lively and incisive singing of the Italians. Once these had finished everyone walked out, and they had to change the order of playing and put them at the end.[15]

The precise rhythms of the Italians, the psychological accuracy of their music, and their clear musical singing, undoubtedly won the first round of the contest. Since they were expelled in 1754, they must be deemed to have lost the last. However, Parisian musical life was permanently affected. The arguments over the respective merits of Italian comic opera on the one hand and of French opera, of whatever kind, at the *Académie* on the other do not constitute the most significant point about the *Guerre*. The Italians made little permanent impression on the *Académie* but they strongly affected opera outside it, namely *opéra-comique*. The controversy also turned out to be excellent propaganda for Italian opera in many parts of Europe.

The Italianisation of *opéra-comique* came about mainly because its creators felt the strong desire to parody the new music. Some young composers parodied to the extent that their own musical language was permanently influenced. Written just before the *Guerre* began, Rousseau's little *Devin du village*, with its Italian-style recitative and some Italianate songs, was the sort of work that stimulated other composers to write more in the Italian vein. During the *Guerre*, *La serva padrona* was translated into French and performed with spoken dialogue replacing the recitative. Here was a perfect model for a new style of *opéra-comique*.

The Italian influence was strengthened furthermore by the arrival in Paris in 1757 of the Neapolitan composer Egidio Duni. He had already had his first experience of writing *opéra-comique* at Parma under du Tillot's patronage, and was to provide many such works for the Parisian stage. Duni was the first of a number of Italian composers to come to Paris in the later part of the eighteenth century to contribute to the French operatic repertory. In the same category must be classed the Belgian André Grétry, one of the finest of *opéra-comique* composers, who was trained in

Rome before settling in Paris in 1767 and whose style of melody was described by Burney as 'more frequently Italian than French'.[16]

The chief resistance to change came from those who felt that the vaudeville tradition should be maintained. The fast, sophisticated style of the Italians was in utter contrast to the popular vaudevilles, and the growing fashion for the former meant big musical changes. In some cases a compromise seems to have been affected, both Italian-style items and simple vaudevilles occurring in one opera. Ultimately the practice of performing already well-known airs in new operas tended to fall into abeyance, though composers provided a satisfactory substitute by including simple, strophic songs of their own. Mozart, it will be remembered, wrote a 'vaudeville' at the end of his *Die Entführung aus dem Serail*, a *Singspiel* with spoken dialogue that has many similarities to French comic operas of the time.

The *Guerre des Bouffons* is important, finally, as being the major incident, and moment of crisis, in an artistic movement which was bringing different styles of comic opera closer together. *La serva padrona* was an *opéra-comique* once its text had been translated and its recitative replaced by spoken dialogue. By the same process German adapters turned Italian works into *Singspiele*. Nor was Italy the sole exporter of comic opera, since *opéra-comique* was performed at various Italian centres, in Germany and Austro-Hungary, either translated or in the original language. Gluck had his first experience of setting opera in French at the imperial court at Vienna where there was an *opéra-comique* team brought from France. The very interchangeability of comic opera was now a big factor in its international success.

But however international it now appeared, comic opera still harboured musical elements that could be exploited if necessary for their national qualities or associations. Most types of comic opera had simple, popular tunes either in a local or foreign idiom. Mozart's 'Wer ein Liebchen hat gefunden' from *Die Entführung*, for instance, is an imitation of a Neapolitan-style song introduced perhaps for its evocation of an exotic atmosphere. Such tunes, whether traditional airs or not, were usually introduced for their musical attractiveness, though the case of *The Beggar's Opera* shows at once that they could also be an aid to nationalist or political propaganda of some kind. In the French Revolutionary period such political overtones were common in opera. Furthermore, traditional and popular song was

by this time being more systematically employed than it had been
in the immediate past as a basis for the development of new,
national styles of music. Opera shows this trend early, especially
in countries such as Russia and Germany. The *Lieder* in many late
eighteenth-century German *Singspiele* were the immediate predecessors of those in Weber's *Der Freischütz* and other highly
Germanic operas of the early nineteenth century, and through these
and other channels had their influence on German romantic music
in general.

1   cf. the appearance of a 'false Venus' in Molière's play *Les amants mag-
    nifiques*, IV ii.

2   H. Goldschmidt, *Studien zur Geschichte der italienischen Oper im 17.
    Jahrhundert*, Leipzig, 1901, p. 121.

3   B. Croce, *I teatri di Napoli*, Bari, 1947, pp. 138 ff.

4   G. Cucuel, *Les créateurs de l'opéra-comique français*, Paris, 1914, pp. 18 ff.

5   Ibid., p. 27.

6   Ibid., p. 20

7   cf. F. Kidson, *The Beggar's Opera, its predecessors and successors*, Cambridge,
    1922, p. 66.

8   C. Girdlestone, *Jean-Philippe Rameau*, London, 1957, pp. 399 ff.

9   cf. M. Scherillo, *L'opera buffa napoletana durante il settecento*, Palermo, 1916,
    pp. 141 ff.

10 Goldschmidt, op. cit., pp. 104–5.

11 F. Algarotti, *Essay on the opera*, English edn., Glasgow, 1768, p. 49.

12 *Correspondence of Thomas Gray*, ed. Toynbee & Whibley, Oxford, 1935,
    ii, 811–12.

13 Cucuel, op. cit., pp. 60–1.

14 P-M. Masson, 'La lettre sur Omphale', *Revue de musicologie* (1945)
    xxvii, 4–6.

15 J-J. Rousseau, *The confessions*, bk. viii (year 1753), Penguin edn, London,
    1963, p. 357

16 *Dr Burney's musical tours in Europe*, ed. Scholes, London, 1959, ii, 3.

PROBLEMS OF MUSIC DRAMA

Understanding of old opera has been somewhat hampered in the past by a lack of easily available published material and by a natural reluctance on the part of operatic companies to forsake the more popular repertory for works whose audience appeal is an unknown factor. The time may come when more scholarly editions, of the quality of the operatic volumes in the *Denkmäler* and *Erbe deutscher Musik* collections for instance, will be promoted and more early opera performed by companies most qualified to produce them. The well-meaning attempts by small, and sometimes semi-amateur, groups should bestir larger companies with more resources to proceed further and present old works as they would originally have been seen. Many a seventeenth- and eighteenth-century opera requires considerable stage apparatus and fine spectacle to make the impression its creators intended. Adaptations of old operas should generally be deplored. Editions not absolutely faithful to the original may be positively misleading to students and others; opera directors should work on the principle that the intentions of the original artists ought to be respected until such time as they are proved ineffective by practical demonstration.

We have already seen how those engaged on creating an early opera formed a closely knit team, producing their separate components to order and often simultaneously, and consulting with each other as the work went ahead. Once again it should be emphasised that all the arts and artists in opera were part of what was considered a cumulative, and all-embracing, theatrical experience. All aspects, even the architecture of the building, were involved. For very special state occasions the ordering of a new theatre went with that of a new opera. While the composer sat down to write his music, the carpenters were engaged on the woodwork and the furnishers on the upholstery. In ideal circumstances opera was absolutely new, and only the French seem with the passage of time to have placed less and less value on the up-to-dateness of what their opera revealed.

The gathering of a team of artists for a new opera meant that everything could literally be conceived and worked out on the spot. Who were the people involved? The Venetian, Benedetto Marcello, gives a list in his book *Il teatro alla moda*, 1720; and since he deals in such perceptive, and usually scathing, detail with the idiosyncracies of so many types of person in the Venetian operatic world of his day, it is unlikely that he has left anyone out. He mentions in turn: the poets, composers, singers, impresarios, instrumentalists, stage engineers and painters, dancers, comedians, tailors, extras, prompters, music copyists, 'protectors' of the *virtuose* and of the opera, attendants and custodians, ticket sellers, mothers and chaperons of the *virtuose*, singing teachers, and finally other minor officials and workmen. No mention is there of any opera producer. The person in Marcello's list whose role comes closest to the modern producer's is the *suggeritore*, or prompter, who acted as the impresario's liaison, arranged rehearsal times, ordered props, lit the stage before the performance, and gave the starting signal to the music maestro when all was ready. However, his position was never on a par with that of the creative artists whose names figured prominently in the libretto but his never. The point is that a producer with the function of coordinating the stagework and the singers' interpretation of their roles was not necessary when composers and other creative artists were on the spot to state precisely what the interpretation should be.

Some of the problems of the birth of a new opera are revealed by Mozart's correspondence over *Idomeneo* between October 1780 and January 1781.[1] Mozart himself was at Munich for the rehearsals; his librettist, the Abbate Varesco, was at Salzburg. Mozart's father, also at Salzburg, acted as intermediary when the composer pressed the librettist for certain textual alterations. The value of this correspondence is partly that it provides in writing arguments over details of a forthcoming opera that would on most occasions not have been recorded. It also mentions the people primarily concerned.

At Munich, Mozart was chiefly working with Count Seeau (the
court Intendant of theatres), Lorenzo Quaglio (the stage designer),
Le Grand (the ballet master), and the singers. Quaglio's share of
responsibility in the production clearly extended beyond mere
stage designing, since Mozart reports him as being on his side in
some disagreement over whether Idomeneo should be on board
ship or on shore in Act I, scene viii. As for the solo singers, Mozart
had previously learnt that it was better to write music to suit them
than assume that they would easily adapt themselves to new roles.
In 1770 he had delayed composing arias for the *primo uomo* in
Mitridate Re di Ponto until he had met him 'so as to fit the costume
to his figure'.[2] So now it was necessary to write Idomeneo's arias
to suit the singer Anton Raaff, and to shorten certain recitatives
because Raaff and one of his colleagues sang them monotonously
and were 'the most wretched actors that ever walked on a stage'.

The virtuoso singers of *opera seria* could no more be called to
account by others for their acting than for their musical embellishments and cadenzas. They were creative, not interpretive, artists;
and few librettists or composers would have dared explain too
much of their roles to them. As Marcello humorously put it, a
librettist during rehearsals 'will never disclose his intention to any
of the actors, wisely reflecting that they desire to do everything in
their own way'.[3] The lack of any checks on the singers led to abuse
of the system. Marcello infers that singers made side comments to
the audience during breaks in their arias; Villeneuve that the long
ritornellos were occasions when the singers talked privately among
themselves and passed the time 'en chuchetant, & remuant les
levres et les bras si sottement qu'on ne peut se le représenter, si on
ne l'a vû'.[4] Vocal technique, alas, was too often considered the only
necessary qualification that singers required.

Different conditions, however, are known to have applied in
comic opera; it is also most unlikely that such abuses occurred either
in early Florentine and Roman opera or in operas of Lully's *Académie*.
The idea often expressed in the sixteenth century that both voice and
gesture should heighten the effect,[5] also the *Camerata*'s statements on
the need for good acting, suggest that early opera singers made
every effort to make their actions expressive. Ballet may have
influenced their movements on stage, since they often performed
in ballets and masquerades with courtiers who are known to have
mimed and danced with rather formalised gestures. In early French

opera the influence of ballet must again have been strong. During his first years at the French court Lully was known for his dancing and singing as well as for his compositions. It seems unlikely that the sort of training he had received in ballet was of no consequence when he came to direct the performance of the *Académie royale de musique*. The constant mixing of dances with the choruses of *tragédie lyrique* suggests that the stage production of divertissements and choral scenes was the ballet master's responsibility.

Broadly speaking, composers had to relate their operatic music either to the character acting of the singers or to the general, emotional moods of the work. The choice of approach was often determined by the type of opera and the convention of the period. In many an eighteenth-century comic opera composers seem to have been encouraged to write music that defined action and movement fairly exactly. Mozart's comic operas are first-class examples of how music can, at times, give almost explicit instructions to the singers to make specific gestures. No one could hear the duet 'Aprite, presto aprite' from *Nozze di Figaro*, for instance, without realising that Cherubino and Susanna should at this moment be scuttling about the stage at a great pace. In the early days of Italian opera, too, singers may have been prepared to relate their detailed movements to what they heard and sang. But of composers of this period only Monteverdi seems to have had the genius, first of all to imagine how he wanted his singers to act from one minute to the next and what he wanted them to portray, then to signify his intentions in music. His *L'incoronazione di Poppea* should be studied by anyone interested in how music can affect every aspect of stage action. Monteverdi had not the orchestral techniques of Mozart's period to hand and relied to a greater extent than Mozart on the suggestiveness of his vocal line. But how apt this line is to imply, for instance, the rage and frustrated little gestures of the valet in I, vi; the rolling, unsteady motions of Nero and Lucan in their cups in II, v; or the fawning caresses of the scheming Poppaea in III, v! The whole opera is full of examples like these. Monteverdi's very close musical imitation of natural voice inflections, and his superb timing of the vocal entries—no one was a better observer, and recorder in music, of what human dialogue sounds like—will be welcomed by the good actor-singer. The vocal part gives him plenty of clues as to what his deportment and actions should be.

Rather different from this type of opera is the one with music

concentrating less on dramatic minutiae than on the grand design.
The best cases are undoubtedly those constructed on lines reminiscent of certain Greek tragedies. They have long sections without
much physical action—indeed some scenes have an almost statuesque
quality—and build up their tension either by insinuating forthcoming tragedy or by sudden and catastrophic changes. Since the
galvanising force in the scenario is usually the clash between human
and superhuman agencies to a point where they cannot immediately
be reconciled, music plays its part best by emphasising conflict in
every way possible: contrasting the gay mood of one scene with the
gloom of the next, heightening the solitary position of the hero by
having him sing in contrast with a large chorus, etc. Characterisation of individual parts may be achieved by isolating and therefore
contrasting their styles. There is no need in this type of drama for
the music to suggest too detailed a series of gestures. Such music
might sound fussy and lacking in the appropriate monumental
quality.

The finest *tragédies lyriques* enter this particular category of opera,
as does Monteverdi's *Orfeo*. Here also we must mention Gluck's
reform operas with Italian text, of which *Orfeo ed Euridice* and
Alceste are the best, together with his later grand operas composed
for Paris. Our inclusion of these operas by Gluck within this
category will be shown to be justified, first of all, if we glance at
the scenarios. In his *Alceste*, 1767, Apollo agrees to spare the life of
Admeto if another will die for him. Admeto's wife, Alceste, is the
only one to promise to sacrifice herself for his sake. In this simple
situation lies the source of several later conflicts. Her love is made
sharply to contrast with the callousness of others and with the cold,
impersonal attitude of heaven. Her promise involves her in emotional entanglements with her husband who, on hearing the price he
must pay for his survival, naturally feels he must die himself. In
Iphigénie en Aulide, 1774, Gluck's first grand opera in French, the
oracle foretells Iphigénie's death before the Greeks may sail for Troy,
and both her father, Agamemnon, and her lover, Achilles, try in
their separate ways to circumvent this prophesy. In these and other
Gluck operas the conflict between what heaven orders and human
hearts dictate seems so irreconcilable that it can no more be satisfactorily resolved than the question of what happens when an
irresistible force meets an immovable object. The happy endings,
arranged by having the gods change their decree, are unconvincing

and were one of the points in Gluck's operas most criticised during
his lifetime.

Gluck's music is fundamentally concerned with the exploitation
of the various possible conflicts, be they in or around a character,
between characters, or between characters and fate. One important
aid was the chorus which acquires a stronger personal identity here
than is usual in eighteenth-century opera and which also contrasts
excellently with individual characters, nowhere better than in Act
II of *Orfeo* when the chorus of devils opposes Orpheus' descent into
Hades. Musically this is represented by alternating sections for the
hero and the chorus, each accompanied by a separate orchestra.
The barbarousness of the chorus contrasts with the more refined,
lyrical style of Orpheus' music; and it is interesting that in other
operas the chorus is again represented as a barbarous faction
opposite the character whose thoughts are of humanity and
love.

The simpler the story and dramatic situation, the better Gluck's
music tends to be. Where, as so often happens, the characters have
plenty of time to analyse and state their feelings, the composer is
able to concentrate wholeheartedly on the expression of powerful,
monumental emotions. His use of the strings to accompany the
vast majority of recitatives—there are still a few recitatives accompanied by just *basso continuo* in the Italian *Alceste*, 1767—does not
mean that his recitative is always lyrical or *arioso* in style, but it does
mean that whenever the expression demands, the orchestra is there
to give due weight and colour to the phrase or passage concerned.
The style of his recitative remains Italian even in his grand operas in
French; the bar-lengths are regular as in Italian recitative, not
irregular as in Lullian. Similarly the songs of these French operas
remain essentially Italian in idiom and many would not be out of
place in an *opera seria*. It should be remembered that in the periods
before and between the creation of his first reform works, Gluck had
composed operas constructed on the Metastasian principle. A
different dramatic plan in opera did not necessarily demand a totally
different musical style. His famous preface to *Alceste* suggests that
he objected to the typical Italian aria of his contemporaries because
its *da capo* repeat was too often an occasion for senseless vocal
display. However, this does not mean that he was himself to ban
da capo arias entirely from his later work. Indeed such arias, sung
without excessive ornament according to his wish, could be more

expressive in operas on the Lullian plan than in Metastasian opera where they were virtuoso concert items.

Whatever the faults in the Metastasian system of recitative-aria alternations, the system itself was not a major stumbling block to suitable musical characterisation. Handel was one who understood well how to distinguish characters in *opera seria* by giving them individual aria styles. Mozart's keenness to know his singers shows how the musical style of a part could be woven around the particular vocal and acting gifts of the singer concerned. However, most composers of *opera seria* and of earlier Venetian opera seem to have worked on the rather different principle that music should depict situations and feelings independent of the character involved.

To explain this point further we should refer once again to the theory of affections.* The idea that music should 'put something across', should communicate some emotion to the listener, may still be found attractive nowadays and can perhaps be defended on the grounds that it encouraged the composer to regard music as an emotional art and himself as an intimate part of his society. There were snags, however, in the assumption that music could, if the right techniques were applied, make humans react in a given way. Some eighteenth-century theorists gave details of how specific emotions could be simulated, and human beings affected, through particular harmonies, rhythms, pitch intervals, ornaments, phrasing and tonality.[6] This type of theory gradually lost favour in the second half of the eighteenth century once the recording of personal sensations and impressions became an accepted part of music criticism, and once music was held to be a matter of individual, not universal, experience. But the theory of affections had long before had its influence on dramaturgical method. It had led composers to strive not for musical portrayal of character but for music with a clear, distinctive emotional content, each song expressing one chief affection. It did not allow for music with an ambiguous or double meaning. Perhaps for this reason seventeenth- and eighteenth-century composers seldom employed recurring or reminiscence motives that might, because of a change in the drama, give a different effect the second time from the one produced at first hearing. They sometimes used musical material on two quite separate occasions in an opera if one of these was the overture. They did not deliberately repeat a song for the sort of dramatic effect

*See pp. 48–9.

found in operas by Bizet, Verdi, and other nineteenth-century composers. There is nothing in eighteenth-century opera to equal, for instance, 'La donna è mobile', the Duke's song in Verdi's *Rigoletto*, which sounds gay and carefree the first time it comes but which acquires on later occasions during the drama more sinister connotations.

The theory of affections was no help either when the scenario demanded the simultaneous representation in music of more than one emotion or dramatic idea. Gluck's 'Le calme rentre dans mon cœur' from Act II of *Iphigénie en Tauride*, 1778, is rightly famous for the way the syncopated notes of the violas betray, in spite of the singer's outward protestations of being at peace with himself, his inner agitation. This musical double meaning is exceptional for Gluck. An examination of his various vocal solos and ensembles shows that he normally created the suggestion of conflicting emotions by placing different-style musical phrases in close proximity or by antiphonal devices. Employing these techniques he was merely following time-honoured methods of obtaining musical contrast. When seventeenth- and eighteenth-century composers wrote duets and vocal ensembles, they tended to ignore any differences of opinion expressed by the characters who were singing together. The extent of composers' capabilities to suggest an argument or dispute is exemplified by the music below in which Venus is urging Adonis to join a hunting expedition while he is energetically declining. At least some impression of conflict is created in this particular duet by the overlapping vocal phrases. These are nevertheless similar in style, and no one would guess that there is disagreement but for the words.

Ex 16   *Blow*, Venus and Adonis, *1682? from Act I*
                         (*MS British Museum Add. 22100*)

continued/

The technical means of suggesting simultaneous contrast or conflict was outside the grasp of most seventeenth-century composers, but later manifested itself in eighteenth-century comic opera—the most experimental genre and the one the least hidebound by theory. The musical examples below from a duet in François Philidor's charming *opéra-comique*, *Tom Jones*, 1765, demonstrate the point. In this duet Western scolds his daughter Sophie because she objects to marrying the man of his choice. As is usual in nearly all duets in early opera, the one character starts before the other:

Philidor, Tom Jones, II, ix
(*Publ. Bernard, Paris, 1766?*)

Sophie now enters, but sings in a manner quite different from
Western's:

Ex 18

The music then develops further round the contrasting styles of the two soloists:

Ex 19

continued/

Both the quaver patter of Western's part and the halting, pathetic phrases of Sophie's are regular 'comic' touches in opera of the period. The interesting thing is that, joined together, they interact in the same way as strings and wind. This gives a clue as to how such simultaneous contrasts were originally obtained. Baroque scoring of the late seventeenth and early eighteenth centuries requires wind and strings to play the same, contrapuntal style of music. During the eighteenth century new methods of orchestration gradually emerged. These included the use of slow notes in the wind—against faster notes in the strings—to bind the over-all texture and provide more variable colour effects. Similarly, slow-over fast-note patterns came to be employed to distinguish different characters in an ensemble. There is thus some evidence to suggest that advances in orchestration had their influence over advances in operatic characterisation. Once composers were sure of these new techniques, they seem to have welcomed the opportunity to write more ensembles. The proportion of ensembles to vocal solos increased sharply in late eighteenth-century comic opera.

The Italians and the French seem to have been the two nations primarily responsible for operatic developments during the period 1600–1780—though this is not to deny the quality of opera, or the efforts, of other nations. Having accepted the basic notion that music was a natural component of drama, the Italians worked in the belief that music was a challenging, not a limiting, factor in the evolution of new styles and forms of theatrical entertainment. This attitude was the key to their success. Modern criticism of their work must mainly be directed at the way they became too concerned with the vividness of the separate parts of opera, sometimes to the detriment of the total effect. The French, initially sharing the doubts of most other nations about opera, showed timidity in the development of new techniques once they had fashioned their own, Lullian formula. Thus they often sacrificed artistic vitality for the sake of maintaining a firm grasp on the over-all design.

But whatever the dramatic system or the style of music, the quality of opera ultimately depended then as now on something else. We must return to the idea expressed in chapter 1 that music transforms opera into an art-form with its own standards. The outstanding operas are those in which the composer makes his audiences become involved in the drama in a personal and emotional way. The end of *L'incoronazione di Poppea*, for instance, where Nero and Poppaea sing a love duet of such surpassing loveliness that all else is forgotten, is the sort of occasion when we, the members of the audience, become submerged in the world of theatre. It is one of those rare moments which provide a yardstick by which all opera is eventually judged.

1   *The letters of Mozart and his family*, ed. Anderson, London, 1938, ii, 977 ff.

2   Ibid, i, 252.

3   O. Strunk, *Source readings in music history*, London, 1952, p. 523.

4   J. de Villeneuve, *Lettre sur le méchanisme de l'opéra italien*, Naples, 1756, p. 32.

5   cf. M. A. Ingegneri, *Della poesia rappresentativa & del modo di rappresentare le favole sceniche*, Ferrara, 1598, pp. 76–8.

6   cf. R. Schäfke, 'Quantz als Ästhetiker', *Archiv für Musikwissenschaft* vi (1924), 239–41.

BIBLIOGRAPHY

The following books and long articles are recommended for further information on:

1 the date and place of production, with other relevant details, of the most important operas throughout operatic history:

A. Loewenberg, *Annals of opera, 1597–1940*, 2nd revised edn, Geneva, 1955

2 the origins of opera:

A. Solerti, *Gli albori del melodramma*, Milan, 1904

3 seventeenth- and eighteenth-century Italian opera:

A. A. Abert, *Claudio Monteverdi und das musikalische Drama*, Lippstadt, 1954

A. della Corte, *L'opera comica italiana nel '700*, Bari, 1923

H. Goldschmidt, *Studien zur Geschichte der italienischen Oper im 17. Jahrhundert*, Leipzig, 1901

S. Towneley Worsthorne, *Venetian opera in the seventeenth century*, Oxford, 1954

H. C. Wolff, *Die venezianische Oper in der zweiten Hälfte des 17. Jahrhundert*, Berlin, 1937

4 seventeenth-century opera in England:
E. J. Dent, *The foundations of English opera*, Cambridge, 1928

5 seventeenth- and eighteenth-century opera in Germany:

E. Wellesz, 'Die Opern und Oratorien in Wien von 1660–1708', *Studien zur Musikwissenschaft* vi (1919)

H. C. Wolff, *Die Barockoper in Hamburg*, Wolfenbüttel, 1957

6 seventeenth- and eighteenth-century opera in France:

H. Prunières, *L'opéra italien en France avant Lulli*, Paris, 1913

G. Cucuel, *Les créateurs de l'opéra-comique français*, Paris, 1914

7 operas chiefly or entirely by one composer:

H. Abert, *Niccolo Jommelli als Opernkomponist*, Halle, 1908

E. J. Dent, *Alessandro Scarlatti: his life and works*, new impression, London, 1960

R. Gerber, *Der Operntypus Johann Adolf Hasses und seine textlichen Grundlagen*, Leipzig, 1925

C. Girdlestone, *Jean-Philippe Rameau, his life and work*, London, 1957

A. Lorenz, *Alessandro Scarlattis Jugendopern*, Augsburg, 1927

P-M. Masson, *L'opéra de Rameau*, Paris, 1930

G. F. Schmidt, *Die frühdeutsche Oper und die musikdramatische Kunst George Caspar Schürmanns*, Regensburg, 1933

8 musical aesthetics with special reference to opera:

H. Goldschmidt, *Geschichte der Musikästhetik im 18. Jahrhundert*, Zürich, 1915

The following articles are also highly recommended:

E. J. Dent, 'Ensembles and finales in 18th century Italian opera', *Sammelbände der internationalen Musikgesellschaft* xi & xii (1909–11)

E. J. Dent, 'The nomenclature of opera', *Music and Letters* xxv (1944)

D. Grout, 'Some forerunners of the Lully opera', *Music and Letters* xxii (1941)

INDEX

Striggio, Alessandro, 71
Strozzi, Giulio, 76
Strunk, Oliver, 17 n7, 52 n6, 52 n7,
    78 n1, 78 n3, 106 n10, 106 n11,
    128 n3, 160 n3

Tasso, Torquato, 16, 73
Teatro della Sala, Bologna, 38
Telemann, Georg Philipp, 96
Theatres: box system, 37–40; build-
    ing of, 25, 29, 147
Tiersot, Jean, 89 n2, 89 n3
Torelli, Giacomo, 24
Tosi, Pier Francesco, 67, 78 n7
Towneley, Simon, 8, 33 n7, 44 n1,
    44 n4, 78 n4
Traetta, Tommaso, 123
Tragédie lyrique, 87, 90 ff, 123, 134,
    149–50
Tuileries, opera house in the, 26
Tzschimmer, Gabriel, 33 n4

Varesco, Abbate, 147
Vatielli, Francesco, 52 n11
Vaudeville, 132–3, 144
Vecchi, Orazio, 49, 51
Vega, Lope de, 74
Venetian opera, 55, 60–1, 66, 76–8,
    84, 87, 121, 129–30, 152
Venice, opera at, 14, 24, 35–9, 41, 70
Verdi, Giuseppe, 153
Vers mesurés, 46
Versailles, 20, 28
Vianello, Carlo Antonio, 44 n9
Vienna, opera at, 30, 60, 77, 124, 144
Villeneuve, Josse de, 148, 160 n4
Vivaldi, Antonio, 102, 116–17, 116–17
    Ex 11

Wagner, Richard, 12, 40
Walker, D. P., 52 n1, 78 n2
Weber, Carl Maria von, 145
Weissenfels, German opera at, 41
Wellesz, Egon, 78 n8, 128 n16, 128
    n19
Westrup, Jack, 78 n11
Wolfenbüttel, German opera at, 41
Wolff, Hellmuth Christian, 44 n13,
    78 n5
Wotquenne, Alfred, 78 n18

York, Duke of, see James II
Yorke-Long, Alan, 34 n14

Zarzuela, 86
Zeno, Apostolo, 25, 107–8, 112, 121